"Eye-opening and thought-provoking...equally beneficial to business and volunteerism." ZIG ZIGLAR

THE NEW BREED

SECOND EDITION

UNDERSTANDING AND EQUIPPING THE 21ST CENTURY VOLUNTEER

JONATHAN MCKEE
THOMAS W. MCKEE

Recruiting, Training, Managing and Occasionally Even Firing...Today's Volunteers

The New Breed, Second Edition
Understanding and Equipping the 21st Century Volunteer

© 2012 Jonathan McKee and Thomas W. McKee

group.com

simplyyouthministry.com

Credits
Authors: Jonathan McKee and Thomas W. McKee
Executive Developer: Nadim Najm
Chief Creative Officer: Joani Schultz
Editor: Rob Cunningham
Art Director: Veronica Preston

ISBN 978-0-7644-8619-7

10 9 8 7 6 5   20 19 18 17 16 15 14

Printed in the United States of America.

ENDORSEMENTS

"Working as a Volunteer Coordinator for a leading volunteer center can be inspiring, motivational...and challenging. The New Breed: Understanding and Equipping the 21st Century Volunteer prompted me to revisit our mission and clarify my passion for providing effective opportunities for the modern volunteer. The all too true-to-life case studies conjured several "ah-ha" moments which allowed me to fine-tune my techniques to make sure I deliver the best experience possible for my valued volunteers."

Christine Wallace
Community Resources Coordinator
Volunteer Center of Sacramento

"I found The New Breed: Understanding & Equipping the 21st Century Volunteer more than a little enlightening. The information the McKees share is current, thorough and updated. Their style of writing is hopeful and they offer clear, step-by-step procedures and processes, answering many of the "whys" along the way. Their advice is eye-opening and thought-provoking. I believe this book would be equally valuable and beneficial to business and volunteerism."

Zig Ziglar
Author and Motivational Teacher

"Tom McKee and his son Jonathan, have created a wonderfully insightful book to help us all understand and co-create the new world of volunteerism. Every volunteer manager in this country is facing the need to stop doing business as usual and re-think their approach to all aspects of volunteer management - recruiting, rewarding and retaining volunteers. The paradigm has shifted and we must adapt. Tom gives great sage advice in his new book, The New Breed: Understanding & Equipping the 21st Century Volunteer and I love the counterpoint of the fresh, new ideas and approaches suggested by his son. Not only is their banter back and forth very realistic — it's also very loving and fun — making this book a sure way to get inside the heads of the newest generation. Volunteer managers everywhere need to get this book — it's filled with great suggestions for changing the way we do our work. Congratulations to this new dynamic duo!"

Mary Lynn Perry, M.A.
Volunteer Coordinator
City of Sacramento
Board Member—Directors of Volunteers in Agencies

"I've never met a youth worker or anyone else in ministry who has a problem with getting too many volunteers. It's not because of a lack of people, rather the problem seems to lie in the approach. That's why The New Breed should be required reading for anyone in a position of recruiting, training, and managing volunteers. The McKee dynamic duo takes this complex and challenging subject and lay it out in understandable and practical terms. Be careful, though — because if you put this book into action, you just might have too many volunteers!"

Greg Stier
President
Dare 2 Share Ministries

"Jonathan and Tom have teamed together to present a very practical and fun book to read. I cannot think of anything more important in ministry or business than volunteers. The book contains not only valuable ministry enhancing principles but is also filled with stories of real people. The resources section alone is worth the price of the book."

Les Christie
Chair, Youth Ministry Department
William Jessup University

"The world of volunteerism has changed a lot over the past ten years and the McKee's definitely get it. In this very practical leadership book, they have perfectly described today's 'new breed' of volunteers and reveal recruiting secrets that will not only help you build a team but keep it together for a long long time."

Wayne Rice
Co-founder, Youth Specialties
Founder, Understanding Your Teenager Seminars

"Leading volunteers has always been among the most vital tasks in ministry. Yet as society has changed, and people's lives have become more chaotic and fragmented, the task of leading leaders has never been more challenging. In The New Breed, Tom and Jonathan McKee offer us all a comprehensive, thorough and usable handbook for equipping and training volunteers in today's hectic world. Wellresearched, solidly grounded and filled with practical tips and tools, The New Breed is sure to become the standard for raising up and leading a new generation of volunteers."

Chap Clark , Ph.D.
Professor of Youth, Family, and Culture
Fuller Theological Seminary
President, ParenTeen.com
Senior Editor, Youthworker Journal

"I have not seen a more effective book on working with volunteers. The New Breed is practical, relevant, and the generational insight of a Father/Son team is very helpful. I highly recommend this book."

Jim Burns, Ph.D.
President, HomeWord

"Excellent book! It's packed with practical advice on how to recruit, motivate and retain volunteers as well as how to keep them happy and productive. It's a quick read and well worth every minute of your time."

Vicki Hitzges
Corporate Motivational Speaker

ACKNOWLEDGMENTS

TOM I would never have been able to write this book without three significant people in my life:

My father. My dad was an eagle scout, scout master, a Sunday school superintendent, and when I was in high school he quit his job as a carpenter to become the director of education and business manager of our growing church. He had moved from a volunteer who spent most of his time at the church to joining the church staff to recruit and manage the volunteers. Dad was the ultimate recruiter and motivator of volunteers. When I got my first job recruiting and managing volunteers (I was 20 at the time) I would call and visit my dad each week with thousands of questions. He was my mentor.

My youngest son, Jonathan. Jonathan was high energy when he came out of the womb. Today he probably would have been labeled A.D.H.D. He always had a passion for people and was volunteering for school and church activities. When he graduated from college and married Lori, they began volunteering to impact the lives of teenagers. He soon left his job selling life insurance to work full time for Campus Life—a position that forced him to recruit, motivate, manage and sometimes even fire volunteers. In those early years of his ministry we would often talk for hours about working with volunteers. I thought at the time, "Wow, we are my father's legacy."

I had written most of this book about five years ago, but I could not get it off the ground and written the way people would want to read it. Jonathan had already published four other books at that time, so I went to him and asked him if he would like to co-author this book with me, adding the perspective of a whole new younger generation that is ready to volunteer. In a weaker moment he jumped at the opportunity and his addition, bantering, stories, and view point have made this book not only possible, but they turned it into something people will want to read!

My wife, Susie: I could never have written this book without Susie's support, encouragement and tireless hours of manuscript reading. She has always been an active volunteer and would bring her concerns and questions about the reality of what I was trying to say.

I could not have written this book alone.

JONATHAN I have to give "big ups" to my dad for bringing me into this project. As a huge fan of free resources for the non-profit, I've always been a big advocate of his free resources at VolunteerPower.com. When he invited me to help him with this project, I was excited to work together on a tool to help the nonprofit recruit, manage, and lead volunteers.

Much love to my family for putting up with me during the writing of this book. My wife Lori is a saint. And Alec, Alyssa, and Ashley all put up with me during the many hours I holed up in our home office to pound this out. I owe them some big time Mongolian Grill the day this is released!

Thanks also to all the youth workers from TheSource4YM.com who shared their input with me about their volunteers—that information from the field was invaluable. A special shout out to Brandon, Lane, Vicki, Sue, Jeannette, Eric, David, Mike, Dan, Angela, Mikel, Rob, Furby, KJ, Danette, and Teddi.

And I really appreciate the work that Roxy, Scott, and Brad put into this project from Group's end. Thanks for making us look good!

CONTENTS

The Common Predicament: Where It All Begins i

SECTION ONE: THE VOLUNTEER RECRUITER 1

Chapter 1: Who Is the New Breed of Volunteer? 3
A Profile of the 21st Century Volunteer

Chapter 2: Recruiting the New Breed of Volunteers 25
The "Courting" Relationship

Chapter 3: Finding the New Breed of Volunteers (and Not Scaring Them Away) 37
The Seven Deadly Sins of Recruiting Volunteers

Chapter 4: Tapping Into Two New Breeds of Volunteers 63
Retiring "Boomers" and Incoming "Generation Y"

SECTION TWO: THE VOLUNTEER MANAGER............... 89

Chapter 5: Motivating the New Breed of Volunteers 91
Retain Volunteers by Motivating Them

Chapter 6: Empowering Volunteers to Do It Their Way 115
Move From Delegation to Empowerment

Chapter 7: Using a New Breed of Technology 131
Social Media, Wikis, Texting...and the Virtual Volunteer

Chapter 8: Managing or Canning High-Maintenance Volunteers...159
Performance Coaching the Volunteer From Hell

SECTION THREE: THE VOLUNTEER LEADER 177

Chapter 9: Leading the Successful Volunteer Organization 179
Mobilize the Collective Power of Volunteers

Chapter 10: Epilogue—A Leadership Case Study.......................199
A Fable of How to Do It Right

SECTION FOUR: RESOURCES 217

Sample Position Charter 219

Sample Youth Ministry Volunteer Expectations...........................223

Sample Project Charter..226

Sample Youth Ministry Volunteer Application 230

Interview Guide for Hiring a Paid Volunteer Manager...................240

Sample Youth Ministry Reference Form 244

Sample Questionnaire for Virtual Volunteers..............................247

Sample Board Code of Conduct..250

Strategic Planning Retreat—Agenda of Questions 252

SWOT Analysis Form..257

Icebreakers and Openers..258

Team-Building Activities.. 264

Sample Training Exercise—A Case Study: "Symptoms of
Staff Resistance" 269

ENDNOTES **273**

THE COMMON PREDICAMENT
Where It All Begins

Both David and Alissa desperately needed volunteers.

Both brand-new to very similar jobs, they worked for organizations with identical visions, but in cities an hour apart. Their success depended on their ability to mobilize and empower volunteers.

Alissa succeeded.

David didn't.

In the spring of 2012, Alissa and David each began overseeing a neighborhood youth center in their respective cities. These teen drop-in centers served as safe places where teenagers could play basketball, work on computers, get help with homework, play video games, or participate in the favorite activity of teenagers today—just "hanging out."

The similarity of David and Alissa's situations was uncanny. They both served at nearly identical facilities located in urban areas of large cities. Both teen centers brought in a similar number of kids. David's facility had couches, TVs, and computers in an open and well-lit room next to the basketball court. A mural painted by local teenagers covered an entire wall. Alissa's center had a similar room connected to the gymnasium with a high-tech computer station, a snack bar, and beanbag chairs scattered across some old shag carpeting.

Both David and Alissa replaced someone who left.

Both had very small budgets to work with.

Both knew going in that their facility was entirely "volunteer-run." Each would be the only paid staff in the building.

David retained two volunteers from his predecessor. One local mom came in at 2 every afternoon to open the center and "chaperone." Mrs. B., as kids called her, wasn't very relational. In fact, she seemed a little quirky. Still, David could rely on her, and she came in 10 minutes early every day. David's other volunteer, a college student named T.J., grew up in the neighborhood playing in the facility. Basketball was T.J.'s life. He loved playing ball with kids and came in three afternoons a week to do just that.

Alissa also inherited two volunteers from her organization. James, a city employee, got off work at 2 p.m. daily and showed up at the facility shortly after. He usually perched himself on a stool behind the snack bar, keeping an eye on the place and occasionally interacting with kids. Alissa's other volunteer, a history professor from the community college who the kids called "The Doc," ran the center's computer station. He came in two or three times a week to help kids with the computers and with their homework.

A week into their new jobs, both David and Alissa started the process of looking for more volunteers.

David had done this before. A decade earlier, he staffed an entire camp with volunteer workers. He knew the job ahead, so he got organized and began focusing on his goal. Knowing exactly what kind of workers he wanted to recruit, David outlined job descriptions, expectations, and the hours they would work before he ever picked up the phone. He was ready to "fill the slots."

Alissa had some experience with volunteers as well. She served as a children's director at a local church for several years where she recruited and trained volunteer teachers for all grades, first through 12th.

David and Alissa both began looking for volunteers, but it didn't take long for them to realize that things had changed.

They were dealing with a new breed of volunteer.

A New Breed of Volunteer

The first week, David talked with 15 people. He followed some personal leads and some that the center's board of directors handed to him. But for some reason, David hit a wall of rejection unlike anything he'd experienced before. After all, David had a way with people, a magnetic personality, and a gifted management style. Yet every person he talked to didn't seem interested in fitting into David's prearranged puzzle.

Alissa wasn't as gregarious as David. Although people loved Alissa, she had to make a conscious effort to be relational. Yet that first week, Alissa recruited three potential volunteers to help out—just a sampling of what would come. Within a year, Alissa built an incredible team of volunteers.

David and Alissa both came into contact with a new breed of volunteer.

Alissa had success. David, a natural at recruiting, didn't.

What Happened?

David didn't consider the new breed of volunteer. Should you? First, of course, you're probably wondering, "Who is this new breed of volunteer?"

Glad you asked. The 21st century volunteer differs greatly from volunteers David had worked with just 10 years earlier.

Let's take a peek and see why Alissa had success, because her success gives us a glimpse at what this book is all about—the new breed of volunteer.

Alissa hadn't done anything magical. She just called a list of contacts: people who cared about kids, people who loved the mission of the youth center. Alissa talked a little and listened a lot. In nine of the conversations, she heard something that related to an aspect of the "drop-in center." For example: Mrs. Ventura mentioned her familiarity with a popular social networking website that she used to keep in contact with her own youngest daughter in college. Alissa had noticed that every kid in the drop-in center spent hours on this website. So she simply asked Mrs. Ventura if she had time to stop by in the next week or so to coach her how to use this site better.

Mrs. Ventura was thrilled to help. After all, she wasn't asked to give up every Tuesday and Thursday afternoon, attend a weekly staff meeting, and go to an all-day Saturday training session. Alissa just asked her for a one-time session on the computer, something Mrs. Ventura really enjoyed and understood.

Alissa had a similar experience with a college kid named Josh, who had grown up playing basketball in the center. Yet unlike David, Alissa didn't have any volunteers who played basketball with the kids, even though the gym was full of kids wanting to play basketball every afternoon. So she asked Josh an honest question: "Do you have time to pop by the center some afternoon this week and take a peek at our basketball court? I'm new here and I think the kids enjoy using the facility, but I really need an opinion from someone who knows both the area and basketball. Could you come by, play with the kids some afternoon, and give me your thoughts?"

Josh couldn't think of any reason to say no to someone asking him to just come play basketball some afternoon, whenever it worked best for him.

That same day, Alissa talked on the phone with Emily, a close college friend who lived across the country and owned her own web design company. Alissa asked Emily if she'd take a few minutes to log on to the center's old, out-of-date website and help her figure out if it was tweakable or in need of a complete overhaul. Before they knew it, Emily was digging through the web code while still on the phone with

Alissa. As the conversation ended, Emily offered to help rework the whole website. After all, she could do it on her own time, in her own house across the country, during her usual late-night productive time.

How was Alissa able to open the door with three potential volunteers—one of them living 2,000 miles away? No strings attached, she asked them to just come by, "check it out," or "give her their thoughts." These three volunteers liked their little *tastes* so much that they all helped again the next week just to taste it all again. This marked the beginning of three long-term volunteer relationships with the youth center.

Dealing With the New Breed of Volunteers

Somehow, Alissa realized she was dealing with a new breed of volunteers. These individuals aren't interested in working under old management styles. And who are we to tell them they should? After all, what are we going to do—cut their pay?

The new breed of volunteer works well with the new breed of volunteer manager. If you're reading this book, that's you! You might be a youth pastor, a parent coordinator at a school, a director of a community center, a children's worker, a librarian, a museum curator, or an association executive. You name it. If your job involves volunteers, you're a volunteer manager.

We've identified three essential hats you must wear for working with the new breed of volunteers:

- *The volunteer recruiter.* With this hat on, you understand how to recruit the new breed of volunteer, who is "cause" driven.

- *The volunteer manager.* As you step into this role, you understand how to empower the new breed of volunteer, who wants to be led instead of managed.

- *The volunteer leader.* While wearing this hat, you understand how to establish the power and passion of your volunteer team.

These three roles serve as the section divisions in this book; we'll explore each in depth in the chapters ahead.

Quick Notes on Format

Two authors created this book—father and son, Tom and Jonathan McKee. We've included many of our own personal experiences and insights. On occasion, in order to differentiate between us, we include titles bearing our names, as follows:

TOM Jonathan and I will both be sharing, but Jonathan is the better writer.

JONATHAN Yeah, but you're old and wise. I'm just a Gen X brat!

JONATHAN TOM We've also included "links" throughout the book to help you jump to relevant topics.

For example, go to the first "link" on page 00.

OK. Enough glimpses. Let's take a deeper look at this new breed of volunteer.

THE VOLUNTEER RECRUITER

In this role, you understand how to recruit the new breed of volunteer, who is driven by the "cause" of your organization.

Chapter 1: Who Is the New Breed of Volunteer?
A Profile of the 21st Century Volunteer

Chapter 2: Recruiting the New Breed of Volunteers
The "Courting" Relationship

Chapter 3: Finding the New Breed of Volunteers (and Not Scaring Them Away)
The Seven Deadly Sins of Recruiting Volunteers

Chapter 4: Tapping Into Two New Breeds of Volunteers
Retiring "Boomers" and Incoming "Generation Y"

CHAPTER 1

WHO IS THE NEW BREED OF VOLUNTEER?

A Profile of the 21st Century Volunteer

Volunteers don't look like they did yesterday. Yesterday's volunteer programs were designed for a different world. And it worked great—back then. Volunteer managers who still operate like they did in the 20th century are the managers who keep asking the following questions:

- Where have all the volunteers gone?

- Why aren't people as committed as they used to be?

- What's wrong with these young people?

- Why are people so busy these days?

Sound familiar?

At times we've found ourselves asking the same questions. But contrary to what many of us might feel, plenty of volunteers in the 21st century are willing to get involved. In actuality, a whole arena of new volunteers exists who'll get involved and be committed to our organizations and churches. But they'll become involved according to their rules, not ours.

As we approached the end of the 20th century and entered the new millennium, developments and trends evolved that changed the way we need to operate. Whether we like these changes or not, they've produced a new breed of volunteer.

These new developments and trends were like seismic shifts—small changes and adjustments that caused a massive transformation. In nature, a series of seismic shifts often result in an earthquake. In the last 20 years, we've observed 10 seismic shifts that have shaken the world of volunteer management and have catalyzed this new breed of volunteer:

1. **Family Dynamics:** From *Father Knows Best* to *Two and a Half Men*

2. **Isolation:** From community to individualism

3. **Flexibility:** From rigid scheduling to volunteer availability

4. **Generations:** From experienced veterans to novice Gen Y

5. **Technology:** From face-to-face to cyberspace

6. **Professionalism:** From skilled workers to knowledge workers

7. **Episodic Volunteering:** From long-term commitments to short-term projects

8. **Slacktivism:** From hard work to easy, "feel-good" tasks

9. **Micro-Volunteering:** From big-time commitments to bite-sized projects

10. **Speed:** From slow movements to fast responses to change

Let's look more closely at each of these.

Seismic Shift 1

Family Dynamics: *From Father Knows Best to Two and a Half Men*

In 1954, TV painted a picture of the "ideal" American home with a new show, *Father Knows Best*. Fast-forward to the new millennium. The nuclear family has shriveled, and *Father Knows Best* has segued to *Two and a Half Men*, a single parent raising a kid. The days of Mom, Dad, Bud, and Kitten are long gone. Think about how this cultural shift in families affects the new breed of volunteer.

In the early 20th century, many people who volunteered were stay-at-home mothers or retired people—most likely your grandmother or great-aunt fell in this category. This trend continued through the mid-20th century; the volunteer system was designed for the ideal volunteer: a retired person or a woman who had plenty of extra time. In the 1950s, most church volunteers and Sunday school teachers were women. But in the latter half of the 20th century many women began to work outside the home. The demographics of many American families changed from the traditional or nuclear family of Mom, Dad, 2.6 kids, and a dog, to a single-working-parent home. Movies like Steven Spielberg's *E.T.* gave us a glimpse of one typical 1980s American home with the single working mom and her three kids.

During the 1980s, volunteer managers adapted and recruited volunteers from these nontraditional homes, including many single professional parents. The New York Times reported that according to U.S. census data, in 1950, 78 percent of all households were headed by a traditional married couple. In 2010, that figure dropped to 48 percent; changes in life choices are a contributing factor.[1]

Most often, Mom works and, in many situations, doesn't have Dad's hands to help her—so she has much less time to volunteer. TV shows like *Two and a Half Men*, *Parenthood*, and *Modern Family* often reflect some of the various shifts in today's family roles. These new family dynamics have dramatically affected the way we recruit volunteers.

Susan Ellis, president of Energize Inc., writes: "How we define 'family' continues to undergo change. The statistics that began to emerge in the 1960s have continued unabated: high divorce rate (even higher for second marriages), single parenting, same-sex partnerships, older children moving back home with parents, multi-generational homes in which grandparents raise grandchildren, couples delaying having children until well into their thirties. All these trends affect volunteering in that we need to change our assumptions about who is available, when, and to do what."[2]

Seismic Shift 2

Isolation: From Community to Individualism

Many Americans today have fewer close friends than their parents did. Despite the popularity of social networking sites and the constant desire of teenagers to "hang out with friends," Americans overall are choosing a smaller number of *close* relationships, and far fewer face-to-face relationships. Greg Stier, from the youth ministry organization Dare 2 Share, describes this contradiction as follows: "Teens will continue to be a generation that is a study in contradictions, i.e. being involved in the community while isolated in their bedroom."[3] In fact, that picture describes many Americans of all ages today—alone in their homes, on the computer with hundreds of "e-friends." Isolated, yet surrounded.

How deep are these virtual "friendships"? In June 2006, researchers reported a "remarkable drop" in the size of people's core network of confidants—those with whom they could talk about important matters. As of 2004, the average American had just two close friends, compared with three in 1985.[4] But in 2009, the Pew Internet & American Life Project came out with a fascinating new report titled *Social Isolation and New Technology*. The gist of the report seems to contend: *Yes, technology does lead some people to become more socially isolated, but not as much as some have argued.*[5]

Understand that this is a topic of debate in many circles. One side really wants us to believe that social networking is good for our society. The other side highlights the numerous dangers of social networking and other technologies. The level of social isolation is one of these debated facts.

Regardless of where you stand, you can't deny these realities from this Pew report:

- *The average size of American's core discussion networks has declined since 1985; the mean network size has dropped by about one-third, or a loss of approximately one confidant. (Note that this finding is consistent with the 2006 American Sociological Review report we cited.)*

- *Users of social networking services were 26 percent less likely to use their neighbors as a source of companionship.*

- *Internet users are 40 percent less likely to rely on neighbors for help in caring for themselves or a family member.*

- *Internet users are 38 percent less likely to rely exclusively on their spouses/partners as discussion confidants.*

Draw your own conclusions, but the fact is, people today have one-third fewer friends who they can really open up with and share their hopes, struggles, or fears. Furthermore, they don't tend to engage in as many face-to-face relationships.

In 2000, Robert Putnam of Harvard University wrote a groundbreaking book discussing where Americans spend their time. *Bowling Alone: The Collapse and Revival of American Community* described how people have become increasingly disconnected from family, friends, neighbors, and our democratic structures. Putnam used bowling as a metaphor. Years ago, thousands of people belonged to bowling leagues. Today, however, they're more likely to bowl alone.

As people in America choose a fewer number of close friends, they become less likely to be involved in groups that volunteer. That's depressing.

But wait. *Any good news?*

Yes! Despite social isolation, volunteering is actually on the rise! With the September 11 attacks—and then the devastation of Hurricane Katrina four years later, then the earthquake in Haiti in 2010, then the quake in Japan and the tornado in Joplin, Missouri, in 2011—Americans significantly increased volunteer activities in their communities, from 59.5 million volunteering in 2002 to 64.3 million in 2011.[6]

In other words, the places where you'll find volunteers are changing. Twenty years ago, organizations recruited the vast majority of volunteers through local networks of religious and civic associations. Today, volunteer recruiters are reaching outside this traditional volunteer network. In fact, the rate of volunteering among people who never attend church or a civic organization has nearly tripled in the last 20 years. Churchgoers and club members still provide the greatest number of volunteers, but those numbers are shrinking, while the number of *individual* volunteers is booming.[7]

The Katrina and Haiti disasters illustrate this trend of individual volunteering. While churches and service clubs definitely took action, a huge influx of individual volunteers also responded to serve with organizations like the American Red Cross. This trend is new to the last decade.

Seismic Shift 3
Flexibility: From Rigid Scheduling to Volunteer Availability

One factor that contributes to a greater number of volunteers is a willingness to be flexible—many volunteers today demand it.

Kim, a 35-year-old volunteer, is the chairwoman of her company's United Way campaign. Kim is used to "high-tech" endeavors and doesn't want to waste her time sitting in boring board meetings. She says, "Email me what you want me to do and I'll get it done."

Sally, a new board member at her church, is retired. She and her husband travel a great deal. At the first meeting, she shared that she could only attend 11 of the 12 monthly meetings, and she couldn't make the training retreat. While the pastor wanted her resignation because he felt the training retreat was essential for all board members, Sally held her ground. She got the training material in advance, listened to tapes of the sessions, and caught up on her own. Sally represents the new, retired, active volunteer. She is gifted and wants to be involved.

Anthony, a 20-year-old college student, volunteers for his church's youth group. As much as he'd like to help out each week, his school, work, and personal life monopolize most of his weeknights. But that doesn't stop Anthony from acting as the volunteer webmaster for the youth group website. Anthony made the youth pastor a simple deal: "Anything you email me by Wednesday at midnight will be up no later than Saturday night at midnight." Sometimes Anthony works in bits and pieces through the week. Other times, he crams in all the changes late Saturday night. But Anthony is completely reliable as long as he can work according to his own schedule. The youth pastor gains a reliable volunteer because he flexes to Anthony's bizarre hours.

Alan, a busy professional in his 40s, gets up at 4:30 a.m. and arrives at work by 5:45 a.m. He often works until 6 or 7 p.m. Once a month on Tuesday evenings, he attends the monthly board meeting for a local homeless shelter that starts at 6 p.m. The first two meetings he attended lasted until after midnight. Alan felt that the board wasted a lot of time arguing over details when its members should have been doing bigger-picture work. He finally told the chairman that if meetings weren't over at 10 p.m., he'd leave because of his early work time. Some of the other board members frown on it, but Alan makes sure he fulfills all his board responsibilities, and he's a very talented and dedicated board member.

The 21st century calls for a new system and for a greatly expanded definition of what it means to be a volunteer. Rather than always recruiting for specific volunteers to fill existing roles, organizations are empowering a new breed of volunteers to work their own way and according to their own schedules. The new breed of volunteer demands flexibility. Rather than recruiting volunteers for preset slots, organizations ask this new breed of volunteers how they want to be involved.

TOM This "new" trend in volunteering might not be as new as we think. Years ago when I was in graduate school and our oldest son, Thom, was in first grade, we got a note from his teacher asking for moms to volunteer as room mothers. My wife, Susie, worked full-time as a high school English teacher while I took a full load of courses. As we looked at the room-mother schedule, we knew Susie couldn't be available when they needed help, but I could. So I filled out the form, crossing out the words "room mother" and writing in "room father." I received a call from Thom's teacher saying that she'd love to have me help.

I'll never forget the first meeting at the home of one of the moms. Most of the volunteers were wealthy, well-dressed women who didn't work. I arrived in jeans—a poor graduate student living in student housing. The women talked about making cookies and arranging for holiday goodies for the school. I kept thinking, *"This isn't what I signed up for."* I felt completely out of place, even though the women were gracious and tried to find a place for me.

When I got home, I called Thom's teacher and told her I'd love to volunteer to help in the classroom, attend field trips, and perhaps even bring my guitar to the class and lead the group in a singing-and-story time. But I didn't think these home meetings were a good fit. The teacher quickly changed the program and classified me as the room father. I had a great year volunteering because the school was willing to let me use my strengths and be in the classroom when it fit our busy schedule. But I certainly didn't fit the mold of the stay-at-home moms who organized class parties and baked cookies.

Through this experience, I witnessed the flexibility of a shrewd volunteer manager. She adapted her program to me, allowing a shift from "you have to fit into our program" to "we can change our program to your strengths and time to help us fulfill our mission."

Seismic Shift 4

Generations: From Experienced Veterans to Novice Gen Y

The 21st century has introduced a whole new set of volunteers, the generation that many call Millennials. This generation of young people, born after 1981, is also called Gen Y, or what we call "The Texting Generation." Many volunteer recruiters and managers ignore these potential volunteers, but that's a huge mistake.

JONATHAN The Texting Generation (Gen Y) is an interesting breed. They'll answer their cell phones in the middle of meetings or lunch appointments. Like Gen X (born 1965-1981), they'll wear torn jeans and T-shirts to your fund-raising dinners. Almost a third of them have a body piercing somewhere other than their ears (compared to 22 percent of Gen X).[8] They prefer texting to talking on the phone. They constantly seek times to just "hang out" with each other. But these teenagers and 20-somethings—raised on MTV reality shows, social media, and video games—willingly volunteer if they think they can make a difference.

Many of these Millennials get a bad rap. They're often stereotyped as narcissistic or entitled. Older generations struggle to understand their mindset. To a young professional in the workplace, "loving what I do" trumps a large salary. Nick Shore, in his 2012 Media Post article about Millennials, contends that half of Millennials would "rather have no job than a job they hate." In addition, they want to be recognized for what they bring to the company, with "a desire to have their tech skills and savvy tapped by senior managers."[9]

- 76 percent believe "my boss could learn a lot from me"

- 65 percent believe "I should be mentoring older co-workers when it comes to tech and getting things done"

When I think of Gen Y, I think of a volunteer named Spencer. He was extremely busy, but he loved his church's college group and wanted to help. Spencer didn't want to attend meetings or even commit to a weekly program, but he was a wiz on the computer and offered his services where needed.

The college pastor shared several places where he might volunteer, but Spencer didn't find any of them interesting. Just when the pastor was about to give up, Spencer asked him, "Do you know how to use a social networking site for marketing?"

Within a half hour, Spencer was giving the youth staff a tour through the cyberworld of college kids within a 20-mile radius. Spencer showed them doors of opportunity for marketing outreach events, contacting students from different campuses, and even creating their own pages within some of these social networks.

The pastor didn't know much about it, but he took a chance, letting Spencer run with it. Spencer worked his own hours (often midnight to 2 a.m. several nights a week). Within weeks, students showed up at the church college group as a result of Spencer's online invitation.

Gen Y volunteers might not always like your ideas. But don't hold that against them, because some of their ideas are better. They are indeed individuals—individuals who often enjoy the community that volunteering offers.

JONATHAN **TOM** Is Gen Y really different from Gen X? Is Gen Y really much different from when Boomers (born 1946-1964) were "20-somethings" proclaiming, "Don't trust anyone over 30"? These are questions that we dive into in Chapter 4. We believe that a whole new group of retiring Boomers and a group of Gen Y's represent an untapped resource of people who are ready and available if we only know how to reach them.

Seismic Shift 5

Technology: From Face-to-Face to Cyberspace

One of the most dramatic developments greatly influencing volunteer management is the Internet. The Internet and smartphones open doors to entirely new avenues of volunteering that cross all geographical borders. We can use these practical tools to enhance our existing volunteer program, and we can now recruit a new type of volunteer that never existed before—the virtual volunteer.

We can probably thank Web 2.0 for the rise of the virtual volunteer.

TOM Marilyn Pratt, who calls herself an evangelist for online networks, startled her audience by saying, "Email is old school. Web pages are so last century." Then she asked the audience of several hundred how many had ever heard of Web 2.0, and less than half the people raised their hands. I have to admit—I didn't raise mine. I wasn't familiar with the term at all. But that's no surprise, because I'm not an early adopter. When everyone else on my block had a microwave, I was still heating up meals on my good ol' stove.

JONATHAN I can vouch for that!

I was the last one to get a cell phone, a PDA, an iPod® , a GPS, an HDTV, and a Blu-ray player. I usually go boldly forward when everyone else has already made the change.

As I sat there in that workshop, in Chicago in June 2007, listening carefully to Marilyn tell us about this tool that had been around for several years, it was no surprise that I hadn't heard of it before. But after only a few minutes sharing the stage with Marilyn, community manager/SAP developer network, I was intrigued, especially when she demonstrated the potential of this tool.

Her workshop followed my presentation about the new breed, during which I proposed that we have to change the way we recruit and lead the 21st century volunteer. But Marilyn took my presentation to a whole new level with Web 2.0.

Web 2.0, simply put, is an online location where users can interact and collaborate with each other about an idea. Forget cluttered email chains, phone calls, and ancient yellow pieces of binder paper with ink smudges. Replace these outdated tools with one simple-to-use central website where a group can post documents, lists, links, pictures, and more, sharing resources and ideas to achieve a goal.

But as I listened I had a major concern. Wasn't this premature for me when I hadn't even mastered email? *I'm barely caught up with Web 1.0!* This is a valid concern, but Marilyn answered my objection when she claimed that Web 2.0 isn't just for the geeks or "first on the block" entrepreneurs. And it is not just our younger generation that is using Facebook® , YouTube® , blogs, and Twitter® . Many boomers who are retiring are tech-savvy and love to get involved in making a difference through technology.

15

To read more about virtual volunteers and using technology to enhance your volunteer program, go to "Chapter 7: Using a New Breed of Technology."

Seismic Shift 6

Professionalism: From Skilled Workers to Knowledge Workers

In the 1980s the rise of the knowledge worker not only changed the workplace; it also affected volunteer management. A knowledge worker is someone who wants to make decisions. Knowledge workers want to be empowered. They want to volunteer, but they want to influence how the volunteer project should be accomplished. Many volunteers today are professionals and want to be treated like professionals.

Tim, a volunteer as a board member for a youth ministry organization, is a computer programmer by trade. He's meticulous, incredibly organized, and insanely busy. But whenever the organization has computer questions or tech needs, Tim loves to help. Tim hasn't always been so eager to help out. He previously worked for two other volunteer organizations, but each left a bad taste in his mouth.

Tim never brags about it, but he's worth about $300 an hour. He can't stand having his time wasted—and that's exactly what the other two organizations did. They didn't provide some of the basic preparations that Tim needed to get the job done right, and they didn't follow through with promises they made. In short: They were unprofessional. Tim hates "unprofessional." So he took his $300-an-hour skills where they were appreciated and put them to good use.

Tim provides a perfect example of a knowledge worker. He wants to be empowered and treated like a professional. If we fail to remember this, we might lose valuable assets like Tim.

🖑 *To read more about empowering volunteers, go to "Chapter 6: Empowering Volunteers to Do It Their Way."*

Seismic Shift 7

Episodic Volunteering: From Long-Term Commitments to Short-Term Projects

Some volunteer managers report that about 75 percent of their volunteers are episodic, way up from the 25 percent it was 25 years ago. Episodic volunteers prefer short-term volunteer projects to long-term commitments. This trend is here to stay, and many volunteer managers are taking advantage of using the episodic volunteer as a "first date." (See "Chapter 2: Recruiting the New Breed of Volunteers.")

A study by the Corporation for Community and National Service, *Volunteer Growth in America: A Review of Trends in Volunteering Since 1974*, reported the following:

> While volunteering rates appear to be at a 30-year high today, the last 15 years also suggest some change in how people volunteer. According to our findings, episodic volunteering (serving 99 or fewer volunteer hours in a year) has increased since 1989....The critical role that time constraints have on the potential for people to volunteer may help to explain the reason why episodic volunteering became more common between 1989 and 2005. Around the same time as the term "episodic volunteer" was coined, a 1989 survey showed that 79 percent of non-volunteers said that they would volunteer if given a short-duration task....Current trends suggest

many of America's charities and volunteer associations may have taken this reality to heart and made shorter, more flexible volunteering opportunities available to "episodic volunteers"—those who are willing to volunteer, but cannot or will not serve as a regular, ongoing volunteer throughout the year.[10]

 This is very popular for young volunteers. My own kids needed 40 hours of community service to graduate from high school. As I watched my kids and their peers look for volunteer opportunities, one of their first questions was, "Do you have something I can do that would take just 40 hours?"

Chuckle if you will, but don't dismiss this. Can you imagine what local organizations could accomplish with more than 500 students in a graduating class having to serve 40 hours each year? And what if we learned how to use these 40 hours to give them a taste for our "cause"? (Yes, we're definitely going to talk about this strategy some more.)

Seismic Shift 8

Slacktivism: From Hard Work to Easy, "Feel-Good" Tasks

For those who love the oxymoron, you will love this one that is coined from two words—*slacker* and *activism*. How can a slacker be an activist? "Slacktivism" is the ultimate feel-good that comes from the desire to give back to society without actually getting one's hands dirty. Examples of slacktivism including signing Internet petitions, wearing wristbands (awareness bracelets) with political messages, putting a ribbon on a vehicle, joining a Facebook group, posting issue-oriented YouTube videos, taking part in a short-term boycott, or making a small donation for a cause with the click of your mouse.

Although we are insulted by the term *slacker*, and the allegation of such a word gets our defenses up, we have to agree with Nancy Lublin, CEO and Chief Old Person of Do Something. She challenged our resistance when she responded to her negative feelings about slacktivism by saying, "If we really could save the world with a few clicks of the mouse, then only a fool would protest."[11]

Slacktivism at its best can deliver results far more quickly than the phone tree or your small-town gossip. In 2011 Lady Gaga raised millions for Japan relief efforts[12] by selling wristbands. A year prior, the American Red Cross' Haiti campaign raised money so fast, phone companies could barely keep up. Phone companies were receiving up to 10,000 "Haiti" texts per second. As of the writing of this second edition of the book, those $10 pledges by text have amounted to $32 million for the American Red Cross alone.[13]

JONATHAN As a not-for-profit leader whose organization depends on donations, if that is slacktivism, *sign me up!* The bottom line, really, is the bottom line. We shouldn't judge any activism—online or off, old-fashioned or newfangled—by its medium. Nor should we look down on those who raise money or mobilize workers using these "slacktivist" methods. Results are results.

Seismic Shift 9

Micro-Volunteering: From Big-Time Commitments to Bite-Sized Projects

The smartphone won a huge victory in the summer of 2011. That June, for the first time ever, people spent more time on their mobile apps than on Web browsers on their PCs.[14] The mobile apps that smartphones offer have become such a raging success, people have tilted the scales. Basically, more people are beginning to check their Facebook status from their iPhones® and their tablets than on their traditional computers.

So it's not surprising that some volunteer organizations have tapped into this growing arena of mobile "time." What if we were able to harness the hours upon hours that people spend waiting in line, or sitting and waiting for an appointment? Is it possible to harness these minutes that add up to hours of volunteer time?

Micro-volunteering is just another way to take advantage of the volunteering trend in which people are reluctant to volunteer for extended periods of time. Micro-volunteering takes this trend to a new level by offering people the chance to feel good by using their smartphones to make a difference in just minutes.

Jump on Sparked.com to see what this concept looks like in action. Click the button that stays "Volunteers START" and they'll ask you what "causes" fire you up. Click on the picture of a hungry child, an animal, or a poor person with their hand out. Tell them what skills you have (design, marketing, web development). The site will then present a number of current challenges that match your profile. If you log in, you can edit and narrow your skills and interests. Then organizations like Habitat for Humanity will ask you for advice or ideas about a current project. Your expertise helps them make a difference.

Seismic Shift 10

Speed: From Slow Movements to Fast Responses to Change

How fast are you responding to change? How quickly do you respond to shifts in culture? Are you even aware of the changes in culture? How quickly do you make decisions? How long does it take for you to respond to your volunteers' requests? These are huge questions because one of the most significant seismic shifts that has changed volunteerism in the opening years of the 21st century is "speed."

Nick Shore, senior vice president of strategic consumer insights and research at MTV, is responsible for all of the research efforts across MTV, MTV2, mtv.com, and the rest of the network's platforms. He blogged this in March 2011:

If we had to identify someone who is the face of the (Millennial) Generation, the way that Bob Dylan perhaps was for the Boomers or Kurt Cobaine for Xers, then today that face would be Lady Gaga's. Considered beyond doubt the "most interesting person today" by the generation the core characteristic of Gaga is the **speed** *[emphasis ours] and ferocity of her self-reinvention. She is doing in 10 minutes what it [took] Madonna ten years to achieve.*[15]

TOM But speed is not just for the young. We all have become addicted to speed. A few months ago I was invited to dinner by a couple of "movers and shakers" of an organization. They wanted to meet with me before I led a workshop the next day. They had some concerns about how their organization was missing a great opportunity of involving the new breed of volunteers. But it is the age of these men that is significant to this story. One man was in his 60s, and the other in his early 70s. The man in his 60s had developed a software company and had marketed it around the world. The man in his 70s had used Twitter and Facebook to mobilize thousands of volunteers to respond to a crisis. These two men knew how to get it done. But their frustration was that their organization's infrastructure was so layered with bureaucracy and so-called safeguards that they couldn't use their skills and talents as volunteers. Both said to me, "If we ran our business like this organization, we would be out of business in a month."

As I listened to these men ask me what they could do as volunteers to change the culture, I understood. Too many organizations are afraid of change. They are intimidated by this new breed of volunteer who wants to get it done—quickly. In fact, I believe that these individuals are not afraid of the young—they are afraid of losing control.

The Profile of the New Breed of Volunteer

These seismic shifts together represent the biggest change in volunteering in the 21st century. Simply put, the new breed of volunteer drives the program. The new breed of volunteer wants to call the shots. These volunteers want to be asked what they see as the needs in the organization and how they can help accomplish the mission. They have a passion for the cause of the organization but can't always fit into the old mold or organizational pattern. The old system worked well with stay-at-home moms and the retired senior adults. But the new system needs to be more flexible and able to customize the job for the volunteer.

Today, many volunteer managers feel like, "Toto, I don't think we are in Kansas anymore." (Ironically, many of their Gen Y volunteers don't even know where that line comes from!) From the organization's perspective, volunteering might feel a little like a mishmash of unconnected programs. But from the perspective of the volunteers, they feel like they're making a difference and they tell others about the positive experiences with our organizations. Because their volunteer work specifically meets their schedules and passions, these individuals want to get involved.

THE NEW BREED OF VOLUNTEER

Do you recognize people like this in your organization? The new breed of volunteer:

- is very busy, has many obligations, and often volunteers for multiple organizations.

- wants flexibility.

- expects to be empowered.

- won't tolerate working alongside incompetent volunteers.

- is tech-savvy.

- doesn't want to simply make a contribution; the new breed of volunteer wants to make a difference.

- doesn't want to be micromanaged.

Volunteer programs need to expand to include the new breed of volunteer or else they'll face extinction. For you, this expansion might be radical, or maybe you've been adapting to many of these developments for the last decade.

As you evaluate what you read in the pages ahead, take some time to look at your own volunteer history. Do you provide opportunities for the new breed of volunteers? Or are you scaring them away?

You might already be asking yourself, *"How will I manage these kinds of volunteers?"* or *"How will I train them?"* These questions won't even be an issue if you don't have any volunteers. So before we explore managing and training (in Section Two), let's take a peek at an effective strategy for recruiting the new breed of volunteer.

CHAPTER 2

RECRUITING THE NEW BREED OF VOLUNTEERS

The "Courting" Relationship

Have you ever been scared by a used car salesman? They're not always so scary when they first greet you. They're much more frightening when you try to leave the dealership.

"What do we have to do to get you driving home in this sweet ride tonight?"

Of course, whatever you answer, you can expect immediate reasoning to the contrary. In the sales world, it's called "overcoming the objection." You try to wiggle free, but the salesman presses you and attempts to "close the deal." That's the ABCs of sales: "Always Be Closing."

As volunteer managers, we don't have to do this, *do we?*

Far from it.

The best recruiters don't use this kind of aggressive approach at all. Consider what it would look like if people dated like this.

"Hi, my name is Jonathan. Would you like to go out tonight?"

"Well, I don't really know you."

"Let's cut to the chase. I like you, you like me. Let's get married tomorrow!"

"Uh. I'm not sure that I—"

"I'll call my friend. He's a pastor. Do you think I should wear a tux with tails? How many kids should we have? Can we name the first one after my Grandpa Festus?"

Whoa there, cowboy. Slow down a bit. No one in their right mind would use this technique to find a date. Volunteer managers shouldn't either. It's a lousy way to recruit.

Recruiting is actually a lot like dating. Let's look at a much better way to date—um, recruit—the new breed of volunteer.

The First Date

The effective recruiter recognizes that getting someone to volunteer is like the dating process. The goal is to get to know each other before you "pop the question" and ask the person to join your volunteer team. This means that you can't rush to close the deal.

When you find potential volunteers, ask them on a first date. Give them a chance to dialogue a little and take a peek at some of the exciting aspects of your organization. This date might be a tour of your facility, an opportunity to experience getting their hands dirty for your cause, or maybe even a lunch where you share your heart for what you do. Regardless of what this date looks like, prospective volunteers get a "taste" of what you do. And by the time you do "pop the question," you can be pretty confident they'll say yes.

JONATHAN When I worked for a campus outreach organization, we ran weekly events and activities on school campuses. I always needed volunteers who would spend five hours a week mentoring students. I quickly learned that *immediately* asking people to give up five hours a week made for a very brief conversation.

Eventually, I caught on and figured out how to take "baby steps." I started by asking people to help in small ways. I might ask them to work security at an event, to serve pizza, or to pour root beer into 250 plastic cups for root beer floats. The task involved a simple job where they felt needed, but where they also had enough time to get a good look at what we were accomplishing on that campus.

That's how I recruited Melissa. She came out to help me with an event because I needed an extra chaperone for just one evening. I didn't even know her that well; a mutual friend introduced us. But in our first conversation, I learned that Melissa used to help out with the youth group at her church. So when I needed help for this particular event, I called her up and confessed, "I'm kind of in a jam. More kids than I expected are attending this event. I really could use a helping hand just this once. Any chance I could twist your arm to come hang out with us next Wednesday? I know you know the routine."

She obliged. Volunteers like Melissa almost always do. After all, I didn't ask them for a huge commitment. I used this method to recruit nearly all my volunteers. By just asking them to help in a small way, I was asking them out on a "first date."

I always made time to talk to these volunteers and ask them for feedback. That's what I did with Melissa. Halfway through the night I walked over to her during the middle of an activity just to check in on her.

"Having fun?" I asked. (I always made sure that I asked this question during a particularly fun part of the evening.)

Melissa laughed and said she was "having a blast."

I told her how much I appreciated her coming to help out. She was surrounded by giggling kids at the moment, so I added, "The kids love you!"

The important thing is, I didn't "try to close the sale." It was tempting to ask her, "So, would you like to do this every week? Just sign here on line 10!" But I didn't. I took baby steps.

Throughout the evening, I sent a few kids over to talk with Melissa and thank her for helping out. By the end of the night, while I was packing up supplies, she sought me out and said, "I had a great time with these kids. They were great. Some of them talked with me and even thanked me for helping out."

"Really?" I said, with my best poker face. "That's great." I asked her some questions and answered a few of hers. I even told her a little of the history of a few kids still hanging around. She seemed captivated by their stories.

I never asked for help. I just told her stories.

 Think back to the two youth center workers in the opening pages of this book. David didn't have success with his recruiting, but Alissa did. Take a closer look at why. David tried to fill his slots, while Alissa looked for first dates. And with that attainable goal, she got three different "dates" the first week of her recruiting. She simply asked people to drop by once and "take a peek," or jump online and "check out the website" really quick. Alissa didn't use an aggressive approach. She didn't go for the close at the first meeting. She just asked volunteers for a date and gave them a taste of her youth center.

Another purpose of your first date is to notice how your prospective volunteers do. Observe them. Gather information. Casually ask questions. Study their strengths and weaknesses. Make it a priority to talk with these potential volunteers, not to share about your organization, but to hear their hearts. Listen more than you talk. Try to discover what makes them tick. As you listen to them you might catch a glimpse of where they'll fit in your organization.

Finally, don't make your first date your last. The purpose of the first date is to give volunteers a taste and gather information. Perhaps most importantly, your goal on the first date is to get a second date!

JONATHAN That's what I did with Melissa. As we talked at the close of the evening, I set up a follow-up date to continue our conversation. Melissa became one of my long-term volunteers, but it all started with that "first date."

The Second Date

The goal of the second date is to tell volunteers that you'd like their help. Now that they've had a taste, it's OK to present your need. People want to be asked. Be specific. Take the information you gathered from your first date and talk about a possible job description.

The second date also provides a chance to share the expectations or roles and responsibilities you have for your volunteers. In some cases, you might give them a position charter or "volunteer expectations" sheet.

See "Sample Position Charter" on page 219 and "Volunteer Expectations" on page 223.

Be honest. Don't try to minimize the commitment. There's nothing worse than an *"Oh, by the way"* volunteer manager.

CLASSIC *OH, BY THE WAYS*

Oh, by the way, all volunteers pay dues to the national organization. Dues are $150 a year.

Oh, by the way, each year each board member calls 10 donors to ask for end-of-the-year contributions.

Oh, by the way, all volunteers attend our annual planning weekend in August.

Oh, by the way, all volunteers need to be fingerprinted.

Oh, by the way, all volunteers spend at least 12 hours just before the Fourth of July working in the fireworks booth.

And the classic comeback for the weary volunteer? "Oh, by the way, I quit!"

JONATHAN I remember the first time my wife, Lori, came into contact with an "Oh, by the way" volunteer manager.

Our daughter's Sunday school teacher was looking for volunteers. Even with her full plate, Lori happened to be available during this particular hour on Sundays. Every week she saw the sign on the door during pickup and drop-off: "We need helpers." As a parent she felt a little bit obligated to do her part. She really didn't mind being a helper. But Lori feared two things: First, she didn't want to overcommit herself. She already volunteered in two other venues, worked part time, and had plenty to do being a mom. Second, she didn't mind behind-the-scenes work, but she was petrified of talking in front of a group or being in charge.

I encouraged her. "Just tell them what you're willing to do. And don't worry—they won't make you preach on Sunday morning."

So she talked to the Sunday school coordinator, explaining that she'd bake cookies, organize the supply room, stuff envelopes, or even help out in the classroom as an assistant, as long as she stayed behind the scenes. Those are great examples of her gifts. If you need a loyal, committed, hardworking helper who will get what you want done when you want it done, Lori is the perfect person!

The leader said, "Great. We'd love to have your help." She also assured Lori that they'd find something perfect for her schedule and skills.

Lori showed up to help the first week and asked, "What do you want me to do?"

The leader handed her a huge manual and said, "*Oh, by the way,* we ask all volunteer leaders to read this." Lori showed me the book after church (I nicknamed it *War and Peace*). She took it home and started to read it. Later that week the phone rang. *"Oh, by the way,* we're having an eight-hour training session next Saturday and want all our leaders to attend."

Lori clarified, "I'm happy to read the manual and attend the training if that's what's needed. But I just want to be a helper." The coordinator assured her again that it was all necessary.

Lori read the manual and even attended the training session. But the phone rang again the next week. *"Oh, by the way,* we need all of our teachers to be fingerprinted. It's $40. We'll send you a map of the place downtown where you need to go."

Two weeks later, the coordinator asked Lori to be a substitute teacher that week. Lori ran a class of 33 first-graders by herself. (It wasn't a pleasant drive home from church that day. Whew! I can still remember it clearly.)

We began to fear the phone.

I told her to give them her two-week notice.

Still, Lori wanted to be a support. After all, our three kids all attended the church's Sunday school program, and she felt she should help. Lori had a big decision to make. Should she quit, feeling guilty that she didn't keep her commitment? Or should she continue, hating every minute and feeling duped by the continuous *"Oh, by the way"* moments?

JONATHAN TOM What's wrong with this picture? The problem isn't volunteers like Lori. The problem isn't even asking volunteers to be fingerprinted or to attend annual planning retreats. Rather, the problem is the volunteer recruiter who uses the "Oh, by the way" method to snag volunteers.

Right now, you might be thinking, "Wait a minute. I thought we weren't supposed to overwhelm volunteers at first." True. We don't want to overwhelm them on our first date. The first date is about getting to know them, giving them a taste of the opportunity, and getting the second date. But we need to be clear with people before they commit to the organization by presenting all the roles and responsibilities clearly. That includes letting them know about fingerprinting, training, and any other requirements.

JONATHAN
Hey Dad, I'm starting to notice a tension here. Are we contradicting ourselves? We've said that the new breed of volunteer wants to do things their own way. Yet we also say that volunteer managers need to have high standards in laying out roles and responsibilities. If we have high standards, how can we also be flexible?

TOM
That's an important question and distinction. Volunteer managers must constantly balance that tension. We need to keep standards high, because the new breed of volunteer won't put up with leaders who are inconsistent or unprofessional. Yet the same new breed of volunteer also wants flexibility.

JONATHAN
So how do we live in that tension?

TOM
It really isn't that difficult. When volunteer managers listen to prospective volunteers during the "dating process," they simply need to evaluate what kind of commitment they can expect from each

individual. Some people will choose short-term service roles. Others, weekly roles. And even the weekly roles vary.

JONATHAN I see this often in the youth ministry world as youth ministers try to balance this tension. Some youth pastors limit themselves to rigid criteria, only accepting volunteers who can commit Sundays, Wednesdays, staff meetings, and events. That's huge! While it's important to have some volunteers who can make these bigger time commitments, the kids in the youth ministry benefit when other volunteers help in smaller ways.

My friend KJ does this well in the junior high ministry he leads. A few years ago, a mom named Jenny asked KJ if she could help. As KJ talked with her, he quickly realized that Jenny was swamped midweek but had Sunday mornings free during the youth group's class. KJ invited Jenny to visit the next Sunday. She immediately gravitated toward the welcome table—a great example of letting people find their own comfort zones. Of course, KJ clearly laid out what he expected overall with the welcome table—the framework of this role and responsibility. But he kept things pretty broad, just explaining the framework. Within a few weeks, Jenny took over the welcome table—organizing materials, involving students, and making guests feel welcome. Most of KJ's other volunteers didn't want to be stuck behind a table all morning, but Jenny loved it, because KJ allowed her to fill in the framework.

I still speak at KJ's ministry, and whenever I'm there—rain or shine— Jenny is behind that table greeting teenagers, introducing new kids to regular attendees, and signing up students for events. She's amazing.

KJ always needs volunteer staff that can hang out with teenagers and attend midweek meetings and other events. But KJ would have lost an amazing volunteer if he'd built a structure that was too limited to include roles like Jenny's.

Future Dates

After the second date, many volunteers make commitments because during that time, they've observed you in action, they've read information about your organization, and they feel ready to get involved. However, some need more time and might say no. But don't be discouraged. "No" often doesn't mean "no"; it may mean "not now." In six months to a year, you need to ask for another date.

At this point, you might be thinking, "Wow. This process takes a lot of time." Some impatient volunteer managers even decide, "I don't have time to meet with each volunteer multiple times to recruit them."

Here's our answer to this concern: While the dating method of recruiting can sound overwhelming, we need to consider the time we waste training and retraining the high percentage of volunteers who quit when they feel railroaded into volunteering. The truth is that you'll actually be way ahead if you use the dating method for recruiting.

FINDING THE NEW BREED OF VOLUNTEERS (AND NOT SCARING THEM AWAY)

The Seven Deadly Sins of Recruiting Volunteers

It's Tuesday night at the district dental society's monthly membership meeting. A frantic society president stands before the group of about 300 dentists and says, "If we don't get any volunteers for this program, we will assume that you aren't interested, and we'll just cancel it."

Some overworked members feel guilty and raise their hands. Others groan and say, "The trouble with our organization is that no one wants to get involved." Others mumble under their breath, "Good; it's about time we cancel some of our activities."

Maybe you've been in a similar situation. Perhaps you're in the first month of your new job leading a nonprofit organization, and you don't have nearly enough volunteers. So you find yourself staring at the phone. But let's be honest. You don't know who to call or what to say. Besides, it's no fun hearing, "Sorry, I just can't" over and over again.

Or perhaps you're the on-site volunteer coordinator for a ministry. People know you're looking for volunteers. But people see you coming from a mile away, and when you get close enough to talk they've somehow scurried away.

Sound familiar? Don't worry; you're not alone. We've all seen it happen. Sometimes the results of our volunteer recruiting efforts appear to be more negative than positive. We use very weak recruiting techniques but wonder why we get volunteers who quit—or worse, volunteers who we *wish* would quit.

Often, when we put on our recruiting hats, we find ourselves under the gun. We panic because we need volunteers quickly, so we're tempted to use anemic recruiting skills. Deep down, most of us know that these don't work, but we fall prey to them because of the temptation to fill a slot quickly. By committing one of the following sins, we not only chase members away, we also burn them out.

Let's look at the seven most common recruiting sins. But with each sin, we'll also discuss methods that actually work.

Sin Number 1

Expect Announcements to Get Volunteers

TOM At one of my recent Volunteer Power training seminars, a volunteer manager named Linda cornered me during a break and questioned the approach I was presenting. She told me that at their orientation session of interested volunteers, they simply passed around a sign-in sheet, received several sign-ups, and then put the volunteers to work.

She seemed to want me to approve. So I asked her, "Is it working?"

Linda was quiet for a minute and then said, "Well, we do have a lot of turnover. The volunteer jobs are never as exciting as they sound in the orientation. After all, it's a lot of work for no pay."

Linda fell into the trap of Sin Number 1: Just make an announcement and hope people will respond.

JONATHAN TOM Let's be honest. Most of us have fallen into that trap. When you need people to volunteer for a short-term project, you're tempted to try any of the following inadequate methods:

- Just make an announcement

- Just announce the opening in your newsletter

- Just give a five-minute plug in your monthly meetings

- Just do a special mailing touting the benefits for being a part of this special team.

But let's be honest about the results, too. Most often, the results are very disappointing. Not only do you not get *enough* people, you get the *wrong* people.

What's wrong with these methods? After all, everyone uses them.

The answer to that question lies in the word *expect*.

Announcements, newsletters, testimonials, and special mailings are all forms of marketing. If you make positive statements, such as, "we have this great opportunity," these methods can be an effective marketing strategy to demonstrate how your organization is accomplishing its mission. However, don't *expect* marketing like this to get volunteers. Announcements can't be a substitute for recruiting. Sin Number 1 is *not* saying, "Don't make announcements." It's saying, "Don't *expect* announcements to yield volunteers."

Sure, it'd be nice if recruiting were as simple as making an announcement. But unfortunately, the classic announcement method looks like this:

Step 1: Make an announcement (in a meeting) or advertise to get volunteers.

Step 2: Put the few who volunteered immediately to work.

Step 3: Begin fielding phone calls from volunteers who are late, can't show up, or are rethinking their whole commitment.

Step 4: Stress over all of the vacancies you have to fill.

If you desire a lot of turnover with your volunteers, rely on the announcement method. The announcement method won't bring in many volunteers—and even if it does bring a few, it won't always bring in the right people for the job.

So *what will work?* Volunteer managers need to realize that most people don't want to volunteer. Instead, they want to be asked. We need to change our perception of the word *volunteer*. We can't see *volunteer* as a verb. We aren't looking for someone "to volunteer."

When you make an announcement, that's what people must do to help you out—they *must* contact you, or "volunteer."

People hate doing that. So make a change. Make *volunteer* a noun. Look for someone to commit (that's the verb) as a volunteer (the noun) for your cause. As volunteer managers, when we recognize the significance of *volunteer* as a noun, we'll quit asking for people to volunteer. Instead, we'll ask for dates.

To review the concept of recruiting volunteers with "dates," go to "Chapter 2: Recruiting the New Breed of Volunteers."

TOM I learned an important lesson 20 years ago that I've never forgotten. I went to lunch with a man who was a mover and shaker. I asked, "Why didn't you volunteer for this project? I could see your name on it all the way."

I'll never forget his response. Chuck said, "If you wanted me, why didn't you ask? I'd be happy to work with you on this project, but I'd never *volunteer*."

Many people will never *volunteer*. Why? They're concerned that if they volunteer, they might not really be wanted. Again, they want to be asked.

JONATHAN TOM Recruiting is an important process. Consider the old rule of communication: "You need to communicate the same message five times, five different ways, and the fifth time people often say, 'I never heard that before.'" You need to use announcements, written letters, testimonials, and write-ups in newsletters. But most of all, when you recruit, you need personal invitations.

Sin Number 2

Go It Alone

TOM One of the most effective recruiters I knew was my father. He'd lived his whole life in the volunteer world. When he and my mom first got married, he served as a volunteer Scout leader. When I was a kid, he served as the volunteer Sunday school superintendent and was always recruiting teachers. When I grew a little older, Dad became a minister of education in a large church and had the responsibility of recruiting literally hundreds of volunteers to run the education program. Each week, people gave their time cleaning, teaching, working in the kitchen, driving vehicles, gardening, leading music, and coaching in the clubs for boys and girls. While he faced an overwhelming job of recruiting, Dad always filled the slots with great people.

What was his secret? Dad didn't do it alone.

In fact, he wasn't even the common thread among all those people. Instead, he'd established a recruiting task force that met once a month with a list of vacancies. With church directories open, they brainstormed possible people to fill the positions. At a given meeting, they might have up to 50 positions to fill. They looked for more than just two legs and a pulse. They looked for people who were a good fit for the need.

This team served as my father's support group. Each member of the team felt the incredible responsibility and opportunity to work together to run an exciting program. Dad's own list of contacts was small. But with his team, the list expanded beyond who Dad knew, to who everyone around the table knew. I recall him saying something like, "It's not who *you* know. It's who *they* know."

Do you have a recruiting team? Or do you try to go it alone?

I've followed my father's example on many occasions. When we have positions to fill, I put together a special recruiting task force. We operate much like a nominating committee. But the key element is to look at the roles and responsibilities or position charter of the open position and brainstorm possible people who fit that role.

For an explanation of "roles and responsibilities" and the "position charter," go to "Sin Number 6: Ask Busy People to Do Busy Work."

So what will work? One woman in our church, Bev, has a passion for children who can't read. She thinks about it, dreams about it, and does something about it. When she approached the pastor with this need, he had other things on his mind—running a church. But he encouraged her to find volunteers.

Bev didn't put an announcement in the church bulletin (first rule of recruiting). She looked for people who shared her vision. Often, this was as simple as watching how people responded when she began to talk to them about what she did as a volunteer tutor. If they began to ask her questions and she sensed their interest, she asked them on a first date. In this case, the first date involved visiting the school where she tutored. One-by-one Bev began to find people who got excited about the vision.

After she gathered people for this team, they quietly started finding others who would go to local schools and help tutor young children. Each person spent just an hour a week tutoring or working in the school library. Bev soon had 40 adults spending time each week at Earl Warren Elementary School in Sacramento, California.

Eventually, knowing that pastors are always looking for great stories to illustrate sermons, Bev returned to the pastor with success stories of how people in the church were serving the community. Before long, our pastor asked some of the tutors to share their experiences with the church. Bev displayed letters from the students thanking the people of the church. Bev continued promoting her passion, and our church has become one of the most significant sources of volunteers for Earl Warren Elementary School.

So how do you not go it alone? The answer to the question is one word: Bev. You find a Bev who helps you find more Bevs, and eventually you have a bunch of Bevs! Bev not only stands as a shining example of a volunteer recruiter; she also represents the exact kind of individuals you need as members of a recruiting task force.

BUILDING AN EFFECTIVE NETWORK

The key to an effective network is finding people with the following characteristics:

1. A passion for your organization

2. Already actively volunteering for you

3. A clear communicator

4. A visionary

Allow us to go further with this.

TOM Not long ago, I was in the Midwest talking with a group of volunteer managers who were very successful at recruiting and managing volunteers. We wanted to learn from one another's successes, so we developed a list on a flip chart of everyone's best sources of volunteers.

Some managers listed colleges as a great place to recruit volunteers. Others listed churches. The list was a cornucopia of different networks that served as great sources of volunteers for the managers in the room.

But a funny thing happened. No one agreed with the overall list. Sounds silly, right? How can you disagree with someone else's success?

Well, the volunteer managers in that room pulled out the *"We already tried that!"* card from their pockets. They immediately started giving reasons why those methods wouldn't work in *their* organization. Nearly everyone in the room reacted to some of the network possibilities. They'd tried those ideas in their own city with no luck. So to them, those connections were dead ends.

For example, some talked about how their best volunteers were young college students. Others reacted to this and said students weren't dependable. Another volunteer manager raved about the support he received from a local church. However, someone else reacted and said, "I get nowhere when I try to interest a local pastor in our volunteer effort. We've given up on working with churches." Another manager claimed that her best source of volunteers was when a local judge assigned people with DUI convictions to do community service with her organization. Yet others in the room didn't know any judges or see the possibility of these opportunities in their own communities.

Of course, that was the point.

The significance of the list wasn't who was or who was not mentioned. Anyone who thought the golden answer was "colleges" or "a judge" missed the point. The significance of the list on the flip chart was the common denominator. And when you find the common denominator, you've found the key element of increasing your volunteer base 1,000 percent.

So what was this common denominator?

That's what I assigned the group. I told them to find the one thing in common with every entity on that list.

This group stared at the list for a long time, trying to find a common denominator. They couldn't. The list was a hodgepodge of organizations, churches, schools, and even individuals. Nothing similar about the groups, except for one thing.

The common denominator was a bunch of "Bevs."

Huh?

Remember Bev, the woman who filled Earl Warren School with more volunteers than ever in the history of the school? Every group or individual on the list had a "Bev" connected to someone in the room.

As we looked at our list, we began to share about our "Bevs." One person talked about how a visionary in the local aerospace industry in Wichita, Kansas, provided volunteers for her organization. Another found his Bev in a teacher at the community college. For another, her Bev was the judge providing workers who needed to do community service.

When one woman in the group said, "I never work with churches because when I went to the pastor…," I cut her off before she even had a chance to finish. "That's the problem. Never go to the head of a church or organization or corporation to set up a strategic alliance. Go to Bev—that person in the church who already has a passion for your organization. A pastor or CEO sees the whole organization and always looks at the big picture. Their passion isn't your organization. That's good, because if it was, then they should be working with you instead of their church or organization."

JONATHAN **TOM** A recruiting task force is a great way to avoid the sin of trying to go it alone. Don't try to recruit tens or hundreds on your own. Look for a dozen Bevs. Each Bev is a source of 10, 50, or maybe even hundreds of volunteers. Bev makes that branch of your network work. And if you give Bev the credit for that branch instead of yourself, it's amazing what you'll be able to do.

PARTNERING

Some use the word *partnering* instead of *networking*. Partnering with an organization also allows you to build a network of volunteers. Loaves and Fishes, a successful agency in Sacramento that feeds the homeless and runs the Mustard Seed School for the children of homeless families, uses volunteers each day to take care of the meals and school.

How do they get the many volunteers they need? They partner with local organizations—mostly church groups. A church group takes responsibility for one day each month to supply all needed volunteers for that day. Other church groups take on the responsibility of the school, providing retired teachers to teach the children at the school.

Sin Number 3

Recruit Only Volunteers Who Make Long-Term Commitments

The junior high pastor of your church sits across the table and jumps right to the point: "Would you like to spend the next 10 years of your life volunteering three hours each Wednesday night, three hours each Sunday morning, a weekly two-hour staff meeting, and—oh yeah, a once-a-month event?"

How would you respond if someone tried to recruit you like that? Maybe fake that you were stung by a bee? That always works for a quick exit.

Rewind. Try again.

"This Saturday morning, we really could use some drivers for our service project."

"Sure, I can help this Saturday."

What just happened?

The new volunteer is much more interested in helping with short-term projects than long-term commitments.

Dan Taylor from Audubon California told us that the Audubon Society had a hard time recruiting leadership, but leaders noticed that they could easily get volunteers for special projects. "We could get volunteers to plant trees, pick up trash, or lead a bird watch," he said. "But we couldn't get people to help us run the organization. Nobody wanted to be treasurer, but they'd go out and plant trees."

The organization quickly learned the effectiveness of recruiting for short-term projects. The more specific the time limit, the more people they could get to join them for a project. People were more willing to give three hours on a Saturday to plant trees, because that was the end of their commitment. Dan explained, "They don't have to go to a meeting the fourth Thursday of the month to sit there for three hours and listen to things that might not be interesting to them."

So what will work? More specifically, how do you fill long-term volunteer needs that every organization has? Good question. Just remember that short-term projects provide excellent first dates.

Look at Maria.

Maria was asked to be on the strategic planning task force for the Association of Nurse Practitioners in her state. She was excited about the project because of the opportunity to work with a professional consultant. But most of all, the scope of the project gave her energy. The state association's goal was to gain the authority for nurse practitioners to write prescriptions like other states had. Maria's role was to gather statistics from other states. Most importantly, this was only a six-month commitment.

Her task force met for a full day of training and development strategy. She then had six months to gather her information, interview officials from other states, work alongside the consultant, and send out the results to the rest of the team for weekend planning sessions. Then her job was done.

Maria loved doing research. She loved the idea of learning from a professional strategic planner. And most of all she loved the prospect of being finished with her role in six months. Maria not only said yes, but when she finished her first six months, she also volunteered to work with the implementation committee for the same project—which was another two-year commitment. Although Maria only volunteered for a short-term project, her good experience opened the door to a longer commitment.

Don't ignore opportunities like these.

Recruiting people to be part of a short-term project rather than what seems like a lifelong commitment works particularly well with younger volunteers. Many people fear getting tied into a job for a lifetime and never being able to get out of it. They get burned out, sometimes even quitting the organization as a way to quit their volunteer role.

Short-term projects, however, not only open doors to longer commitments, they also expose volunteers to your leadership. Always use one of your organization's most effective leaders to lead your short-term project teams. Volunteers will have the opportunity to catch the vision of the organization as they work alongside a passionate leader.

Sin Number 4

Assume That "No" Means "Never"

"No!"

"I have too much on my plate right now."

"Sorry, I just can't."

Any volunteer recruiter knows these responses well. But don't make the mistake of crossing these people off your list when you hear it. "No" doesn't necessarily mean "never."

TOM A number of years ago, I was asked to be on the capital campaign committee for our church. Bob, the chairman of the board, followed all of the above principles. He invited me out to lunch to talk with me about the need. I really wanted to help, but I'd been on these kinds of committees before. So I knew what a huge job it was. I told Bob that I'd think it over, talk with my wife, and get back to him.

In a week, I called Bob and told him, "Thanks for asking, but I just have too much on my plate right now. Susie said that if I said yes I could look for a new wife." Although she was teasing, she was dead serious about my overcommitment.

Bob was supportive and asked me about what was going on in my life at the time. I explained to him about a new business I was starting, and how I was working all I could to keep two sons in college. I also explained that I had another volunteer board commitment for the next three years.

After that, Bob met with me for lunch occasionally. Three years later he asked me about another position, and I said, "Yes, I'd love to." I think he wrote in his tickler file: "Tom has heavy volunteer commitment that will be up in three years."

JONATHAN TOM *So what will work?* As you can see, timing is everything. When you get the courage to recruit someone and that person says no, you might feel rejected. Instead, try to think of a "no" as an open door to listen carefully to the reasons. Sometimes the "no" just means "not now."

Of course, sometimes the "no" means that the prospective volunteers would rather do something else. When the answer is "no," from time to time you might ask if any positions in your organization interest them, including ones that they were never asked to consider. You might be surprised at what people say.

Sin Number 5

Recruit Any Ol' B.I.C.

As volunteer recruiters, it's also easy to fall into the trap of following the B.I.C. syndrome. We desperately need a volunteer, so we plead our case to anyone with a pulse. We lower our standards, and at the last minute we get someone to be a B.I.C. A B.I.C. is a "Butt In the Chair." However, most times we realize that the chair would have been better empty than filled with the wrong butt. Most of us have had a few of these "butts" on our teams!

Another variation of the B.I.C. method is just to say, "Please come and be a part of our group. We have a great time and we need your expertise." But we don't tell the prospective volunteers what we want them to do.

So *what will work*? R&R. Not rest and relaxation, but roles and responsibilities. Effective recruiting demands a very clear, complete, and brief presentation of the roles and responsibilities of the position you're recruiting for. This not only helps people know what to do once they get started, it also helps them evaluate if they're a good fit to begin with.

Think about this for a second. If we can help volunteers understand the what and why of what they'll be doing and help them fit where they can really make a difference, our retention will increase exponentially.

For short-term projects, the presentation of roles and responsibilities might be a simple but clear explanation of your expectations. (After all, volunteers picking up trash on the side of the highway for three hours once on a Saturday probably don't need a lot of parameters.) But even short-term projects that last a week or two can benefit from clearly explaining roles and responsibilities of the volunteers involved. Long-term positions demand this.

Roles and responsibilities look different in different organizations. A small service organization might have a one-page "Volunteer Expectations" sheet that details the purpose, the time commitment, and a few guidelines. Other organizations might prefer a more professional approach with an official position charter.

See "Volunteer Expectations" sample on page 223.

A position charter provides another great way to give a clear, complete, and brief presentation of the roles and the responsibilities for a volunteer position.

ADVANTAGES OF A POSITION CHARTER

We prefer position charters over job descriptions for the following reasons:

A position charter suggests a higher commitment level.

A charter is an agreement between the organization and the volunteer.

When a volunteer reads the position charter, he or she understands the level of commitment expected.

The position charter raises the professional image of the volunteer position and makes the recruiting process much clearer.

By communicating clearly the expectations for your volunteer positions, your organization's retention rates will increase dramatically. Many volunteers quit simply because they didn't know what they'd gotten into.

See Section Four for guidance on creating a "Position Charter" and an example charter.

Another way to solve the B.I.C. problem is to ask, "What drives our recruiting needs?" Is it the number of slots you need to fill? Or finding the right person for the vacant position?

- "We need six board members for our community center by January."

- "We need five more Sunday school teachers next Sunday."

- "We need three team members for our work golf tournament committee."

So what do you do—just fill the slots? Will any ol' volunteer do? Do you just recruit people who like to golf for the golf committee? What if they aren't good at soliciting hole sponsors or if they feel awkward collecting prizes?

Many of us fall into the trap of committing Sin Number 5. We just fill the slots with a warm body and don't find a good fit for the position. We easily become overwhelmed when we only see openings to fill. The number becomes the focus, and the position takes back seat to filling the slot.

The leader of an after-school teen center in the inner city recruited Joan, who loved doing behind-the-scenes work. When she was placed on the "development committee," she imagined herself organizing, stuffing envelopes, and other various office tasks. But she soon learned that "development committee" was a euphemism for "fundraising." Her job consisted of making phone calls and soliciting support. Although Joan had a passion for the cause, she felt overwhelmed and disappointed. So she quit.

TOM This sin happens often with volunteer boards. Leaders from a theological seminary recruited me, but they didn't fall into the trap of Sin Number 5. In fact, they did the exact opposite. The result was one of the most rewarding volunteer experiences I've ever had. This organization chose board members carefully according to criteria that best fit the position they needed to fill.

In this situation, they were looking for someone to chair the academic committee. When they recruited me, they provided written roles and responsibilities of the very specific committee chair position, and they outlined the expectations of all board members. I accepted the position and thoroughly enjoyed the experience.

Compare that experience with another board that tried to recruit me. As I looked over the list of committees (membership, golf tournament, events, awards, legislative, communications, nominating, professional development, and annual convention), I asked which one I'd serve on. The board chair said that they wouldn't know until they determined who accepted nominations. At the first board meeting, they'd choose who served on which committee. This board was slot-driven. They needed six more board members.

I immediately remembered Joan, who was recruited to be a part of a team without any regard for her gifts or desires. So I turned the position down.

JONATHAN TOM Here's the bottom line. First determine what specific skills (positions) you need on your board or in your organization. Then go and find the people with those skills who best meet your needs.

Sin Number 6

Treat Professionals Like Lackeys

Sometimes we're asked, "Do you ever feel guilty about asking already busy people to become more busy?" People who ask this question still live in the old system of volunteer management. The very nature of this question demonstrates the problem of a 50-year-old volunteering method, because the question is framed around the word *busy*.

We have a very busy family friend, Don Leraas. Don is a husband, father, and grandfather. He's a master electrician, drives 18-wheelers, and works on his own classic Chevys and trucks. He previously served as the project manager for the electrical work on many of the high-rise buildings in Silicon Valley. Don also loves trucks; he'll often drive an 18-wheeler on a quick haul in Northern California. We've never seen a time when Don wasn't busy.

Don also serves as a youth volunteer. He loves kids. He uses his knowledge as a driver to help plan trips for the youth group at church. After his hard day's work, you might find him working with a group of teenagers, designing and creating the lighting sets for their play or musical group. He's also in charge of overseeing all the buses at the church (four touring buses, one fixed-up school bus with chrome wheels, and one kitchen bus), training drivers, and making sure that the vehicles are road ready.

Should we feel guilty about asking Don to drive on a tour for seniors or a youth group? Absolutely not. He'd be upset if we didn't ask him. And no, you can't have his phone number!

So what will work? The 21st century volunteer needs a reframed question. How do you reframe it? Don't belittle busy professionals by asking them to just do busy work.

Notice how we would frame the recruiting question with someone like Don. We'd ask him to be in charge of the transportation, because that's something he loves. We wouldn't ask, "I know you're so busy and hate to ask you this, but could you wash the bus?" Volunteers like Don don't just want to "wash a bus." As professionals, they want to be asked to be in charge of something significant that they also love.

In the next chapter, we're going to look at the two available, passionate, and untouched resource groups for volunteers that represent these kinds of professionals:

1. The huge numbers of retiring boomers

2. The growing numbers of young 20-something professionals

These two groups have something in common. They have technical, leadership, artistic, management, and educational skills at a professional level. In the past, volunteer managers mistakenly believed that the only thing volunteers could do were the monotonous jobs that the paid staff didn't want to do.

And yes, times always exist when we need to recruit a lot of people to do a project of "busy work." These special workdays of stuffing envelopes or cleaning up the building are necessary at times. However, the new breed of volunteer likes to be recruited for a workday where they can use their expertise (carpentry, technical, gardening).

The new breed of volunteers is very sophisticated. Managing, motivating, and empowering the knowledgeable and professional volunteer all begins with recruiting and what we ask these volunteers to do.

Let skilled professionals use their skills!

Sin Number 7

Hire Professionals Who Know Nothing About Volunteer Management

Sin Number 7 is a little different, because it's a sin committed by organizations, not individuals. Many organizations that need volunteer managers make the mistake of hiring someone who is very good at what the organization does rather than a volunteer leader. These experts in the field are inexperienced when it comes to recruiting and managing volunteers.

For example, historians love to study, research, and teach history, but some end up as curators of museums. And what are curators expected to do? Many times their primary role is managing volunteers.

Or take a young minister who graduates from seminary with a Master of Divinity. Most young seminarians know that their major responsibility is to "equip the people of the church," and most believe they can accomplish this through the pulpit. Yet they end up spending their time doing the hands-on ministry of the church themselves, rather than recruiting, training, and mobilizing lay people in the church to do the work of the ministry. Seminaries don't spend a lot of time training ministers to be volunteer managers.

This happens in almost every nonprofit organization because most nonprofit organizations depend on volunteers to carry out their missions. Many of these professionals end up feeling deceived. They never realized that a hefty part of what they did would be recruiting and managing volunteers. And even if it was a bullet on the original job description, they never realized it would be such a huge task.

So what will work? It sounds simple, but read carefully. Organizations that rely on volunteers need to hire volunteer managers for their volunteer managing positions.

Think about this for a second. If a church needs someone to recruit and manage 200 Sunday school teachers, who should they look for? A good teacher? Or a volunteer manager who also knows the trade?

When organizations hire volunteer managers, they should always ask these questions:

- What's your experience in working with volunteers?

- How have you handled volunteers who didn't follow through?

- How have you increased your effectiveness with the work of volunteers?

- Tell me about an exciting experience you have had in working side by side with a volunteer in your past work experience.

- Tell me about an unsuccessful experience you had in working with a volunteer in your last job.

For additional questions and guidelines, see the "Interview Guide for Hiring a Paid Volunteer Manager" in Section Four.

When you're looking for a volunteer manager, you need to begin with someone who has a high commitment to volunteers. This person must understand that one of the most important aspects of the job is working with volunteers. If the person doesn't have experience with volunteers, then you're taking a chance. As you listen to the individual's answers to your interview questions, you should be listening for a "positive volunteer attitude." If you hear comments like, "Well, we should just hire interns if we really want to get this done right," understand that you're seeing a precursor of an attitude that might just be resistant to recruiting volunteers.

When you recruit volunteer managers, you need to be realistic about what the job entails. If your church hires a children's leader who'll be responsible for hundreds of volunteers, this person must realize that a huge portion of the job involves managing volunteers.

TOM Cheryl Lash is the librarian responsible for developing and managing the research library for the Shriners Children's Hospital in Sacramento. I asked Cheryl how her new job was going. As she shared a little about her job, she mentioned that she had several volunteers working with her. My ears perked up. I was curious. I asked if she knew that she'd be managing volunteers when she first accepted the job.

She smiled. "That is part of what librarians do—we manage volunteers." She went on to tell me that volunteering is how she got started working in her field—volunteering in a school library. She then went on to get her degree because the volunteering awakened her passion for library work.

The Shriners Children's Hospital doesn't commit this seventh sin. When you think Shriners, you think volunteer. People who work for Shriners Children's Hospital know they're going to be managing volunteers. That's one reason they're so successful.

Seven Skills

You've seen the sins. Now that you know what to avoid, you can replace these seven sins with seven strong, power-recruiting skills:

1. Ask personally rather than rely on announcements—get the first date. Remember that you're not looking for someone "to volunteer." You're looking for someone to commit as a volunteer for your cause.

2. Develop strategic recruiting partnerships—build your network or a recruiting team. Don't go it alone.

3. Recruit short-term project teams. The more specific the time limit, the more people you'll likely get to join you to help with a project. And short-term commitments might open the door to longer commitments.

4. Assume that a "no" means "not now," or "not this position." Think of a "no" as an open door to listen carefully to the reasons behind the "no."

5. Develop roles and responsibilities or a position charter for each position. Don't fill any position until you find the person who matches what you're looking for.

6. Recruit specific people for specific roles. Ask professionals to be in charge of significant areas of your organization that also represent what they love doing.

7. Hire true volunteer managers—people who know and live out the principles of this book and are ready to devote a good portion of their time to managing volunteers. Make sure they have a "positive volunteer attitude."

CHAPTER 4

TAPPING INTO TWO NEW BREEDS OF VOLUNTEERS

Retiring "Boomers" and Incoming "Generation Y"

We hear this question all the time: "How can we get the younger generation involved?"

In fact, we asked the same question of the volunteer manager at Shiner's Hospital. Her answer was typical. She was quiet for a time and then answered, "We don't, for the most part, except for school internships."

A lot of volunteer managers don't like working *with* the younger generation, and the younger generation does not like working *for* older generations. In case, you didn't notice, the two key words in that last sentence are "with" and "for." The important question that you must answer is, "How do you create a volunteer culture that attracts the growing numbers of retiring Boomers and emerging young professionals—and encourages them to work together?"

For years, I've divided a workshop that I teach into two groups: Baby Boomers (born roughly between 1943 and 1964) and Generation X (born roughly between 1965 and 1981). I always ask the groups to discuss this question: "What are the differences in the work ethic of the Boomers and Gen Xers?" After about 15 minutes of discussion, I have the Boomers report first. I've listened to these reports for more than 10 years, and they nearly always say the same thing:

Gen Xers aren't committed. They often come late, leave early, and work on their own time schedule. They show no respect for authority. They don't want to do any more than is expected, and they'll jump ship as soon as a more lucrative offer is on the table. They're very knowledgeable about high-tech stuff, and they keep wanting to change things. But you can't depend on them when you need to get a job done.

Then I give the Gen X group a turn. I'll never forget when I heard an Xer give the following report:

What you've just said is true. We're exactly what you said because that's the way you brought us up. We watched you work for 70 or 80 hours a week for the same company for the last 40 years, and then that company dumped you. We watched you divorce each other and leave us home alone while you tried to make a living on your own. We were shuffled from one home to another, and we learned to be independent. We grew up with presidents who lie and company presidents who get rich while the rest of you make money for them. We've learned to look at work as a job to support a lifestyle while you look at work as a lifestyle. Don't ask us to work overtime, because we have a life outside of work. Don't expect us to devote our lives to your goals.

When the young man gave that report, the room was quiet. The Boomers looked at each other, and finally one woman spoke up and said, "Wow, what an indictment!" When I asked if they thought what the Gen Xer said was true, the Boomers agreed that it was pretty much right on.

In 2006, I began to change the experiment. I did the same exercise, except the parameters were different. I simply divided the room by those under 25 and those over 25. As the room finished dividing, one side of the room was made up of Generation Y (those under 25 at the time, also called Millennials or Nexters). The other side of the room was usually comprised of Xers and Boomers (25 and up).

I asked the same question. The answers didn't change.

The Gen Xers just joined up with the Boomers—finally agreeing on something—to criticize this new generation. They voiced almost the exact same complaints that the Boomers verbalized about Xers years earlier. The new generation, those 25 and under, repeated the age-old complaints about the generations older than them.

What does this tell us?

I've come to the following conclusion: Most of us simply see the world very differently when we're 20 than we do when we're 35 or 50.

I've been reading about and listening to people speculate about the differences in the generations for decades. To be honest, the complaints don't sound much different. Yes, a 20-year-old in 2012 has some unique differences from someone who was 20 in 1992 or in 1972. For example, most of us would agree that today's 20-year-old is more tech-savvy and a better multitasker. In fact, entire books have been written on the subject. Yet I find that most people who want to compare the 20-year-olds of today with others don't compare them to 20-year-olds of the past. They compare them to the 35-year-olds of today or the 50-year-olds of today.

So what's my point? If we're going to make a comparison, let's not look at generations. Let's look at life stages.

Life Stages

In our research for this book, we surveyed a large number of ministers about their volunteers. We asked specific questions about the differences between the generations. As the responses poured in, we began to notice a pattern. Most people didn't compare the generations to each other "apples to apples." Most of the volunteer leaders in the world of children's and youth ministry compared today's life stages to each other. One of the responses we received from a 20-something youth minister named Brandon was classic:

What I've found with older people is that, yes, they might be loyal to me as a leader. But they view youth ministry or their volunteering as exactly that, volunteering. Don't get me wrong, they love students. But what I've noticed is that if you call them to give more of their free time, they won't do it. Or you have to beat them to do it. I'm not quite sure why, but it just seems that they view ministry as more of an event on a night of the week. Now that being said, the college students are quite the opposite as far as involvement, passion, and their ability to follow.

JONATHAN I loved Brandon's answer—first, because I forced him to qualify the word "older." He replied by saying, "Old like you (referring to me)." After I finished beating him up, I asked him if he actually knew how old I was. He was close. He guessed that I was 35, and I was 36 at the time. Either way—Dad, that makes you ancient!

Second, I loved his reply because it showed the disparity in how different ages view each other. Brandon would rather recruit "young singles" than "married with kids." So was he making a comparison between Gen Y and Gen X? Far from it. Even if he didn't use the term, he was really comparing life stages.

I'm textbook Generation X. When I was 20, I volunteered with a youth group. I helped out on Sundays and Wednesdays, I led a small group of guys, and I regularly had all-night lock-ins at my house. I was 20 and full of spunk.

But now I'm over 40 and have three kids. Let's just say that I've been "despunked." For what seems like the last decade, my wife and I have picked up the kids from school at different times and have taken them to swimming, gymnastics, soccer, track, or karate. In our "spare time," we've tried to get each to their separate school and youth group activities. Once, we even blocked out Tuesday nights just so we could have a family night with no other activities. On this night, our girls skipped swimming and no one was allowed to book any activities. Why? We're overloaded. And most of my friends in this life stage find themselves in the same boat.

This doesn't mean that people in this life stage don't volunteer. Last year, my wife and I both volunteered in the junior high group at our church. And we were just like Brandon described. We volunteered on Wednesday nights only. Why? We were already driving our son there for youth group, and our daughters were in activities in the building across the quad. So we thought, "Might as well stick around and help." But we were too swamped with other activities to volunteer beyond that.

Is that the stigma of Generation X? Not at all. It truly is a life-stage thing.

In fact, a decade ago, I was in Brandon's shoes. I was a youth worker who, looking for "loyal" volunteers, found the majority of them in Gen X young singles. Now those same people—members of that same generation—are "married with children" and less likely to become loyal volunteers for Brandon or any other youth minister.

Same generation, different life stage.

Most "married with kids" people won't volunteer overtime. They're tapped out. Don't call it a Gen X thing. Wait a decade or two until their kids are out of the house and you'll see that it was a life-stage thing. They'll be available like increasing numbers of older Boomers are now.

Two Willing Groups

So what? We could fill the rest of this book with a discussion about generations and life stages. But that doesn't help us get volunteers. So let's cut to the chase: Who should we try to recruit?

The 21st century has seen the rise of two huge groups that are ready, willing, and excited to help you accomplish your mission. If you're not tapping into these two resources, you're missing a great opportunity to expand your volunteer base.

We've hinted at this already, but these two groups consist of retiring members of the Baby Boomer generation and older members of Gen Y. Some of the characteristics of these two groups are purely generational. But even more of their qualities are distinctive of a given life stage. Because these groups are available now as volunteers, it's valuable to examine both their generational characteristics and their current life-stage qualities.

TOM I am going to discuss my generation—the retiring professional culture. I'm just a bit older than the sociological definition of Boomers. But I do represent sort of an older professional boomer culture that is just beginning to retire. So I'll take a look at the best ways to recruit and manage us.

JONATHAN Then I'm going to discuss members of Gen Y who are volunteering in great numbers. Again, I'm a Gen Xer, but I've had a lot of contact with Gen Y volunteers and have made some observations about how to recruit and manage them

Retiring Boomer Professionals

TOM Let's take a look at these older professionals who are at or near retirement. Paul McCartney included these words in his song "When I'm 64":

When I get older losing my hair
Many years from now...
You can knit a sweater by the fireside
Sunday mornings go for a ride,
Doing the garden, digging the weeds,
Who could ask for more...
When I'm sixty-four.[16]

This song came out when Paul McCartney was in his 20s, but he was only a teenager when he wrote it. That's how he viewed getting old—losing his hair, sitting by a fireplace knitting a sweater, going for a Sunday drive, and pulling weeds. But in 2006 Paul McCartney turned 64.[17] This was the same year I turned 64. Although we're not officially part of the post-World War II babies called Boomers who started turning 60 in 2006, I identify with this growing number of potential volunteers. These older professionals are entering their retirement years with an unparalleled *vigor*—to use a John F. Kennedy word. Smack in the middle of the Boomer group are people like Robin Williams (born in 1951), Denzel Washington (born in 1954), and Tom Hanks (born in 1956).

To put it mildly, the retiring professionals of today aren't fulfilling McCartney's picture of the 64-year-old. We're a different kind of graying generation. Walk by any clubhouse of an "active adult living community" (you have to be over 55 to live there) and you'll find that Sinatra is out. You'll hear music by the Eagles and Sting. We're not your father's grandfather.

The young people of the 1960s were this leading edge of the Boomer generation. We challenged the system.

We grew up in an age of growth and prosperity. Our parents worked hard to make sure that they could send us to college. In the early 1960s, we heard President Kennedy say, "Ask not what your country can do for you—ask what you can do for your country." And many of us did just that, volunteering for the Peace Corps and making an impact on the "Great Society."

But in the late 1960s and early 1970s, everything changed. Vietnam, the assassinations of the Kennedys and Martin Luther King Jr., and controversies like Watergate greatly influenced us. Many of us turned inward. During the 1970s and 1980s, many of our generation followed the advice of Erhard Seminars Training and Self magazine and read best-sellers like *Looking Out for Number 1*. And during this time, we were raising Generation X.

Now that we've entered the 21st century, many of us realize that living for self has not been the fulfilling life we expected. In spite of our selfishness, we volunteer because the "I want to change the world" of the 1960s still beats in our hearts. The "graying of the Peace Corps" provides a good example, as people in their 50s and 60s leave lucrative careers to join the Peace Corps and other organizations with social or spiritual missions. Volunteering offers a way to fulfill our passion.

When Paul McCartney wrote "When I'm Sixty-Four," the average life expectancy was 69.7.[18] So he was singing about an age just five years away from death. Now, however, life expectancy is at least 13 years past 64 and growing each day because of medical advancements and innovations. Paul and the rest of us in his "64 club" (including Harrison Ford, Aretha Franklin, Barbra Streisand, and Muhammad Ali) probably don't relate to the picture he painted back then of knitting by the fireside in a rocking chair. And those of us who are in the 64 club all turned 70 in 2012. And as I write this, most of us are not sitting in rocking chairs. In fact, I just returned from a volunteer trip to Uganda and plan on many more volunteer services.

I'm not alone: Many of my friends in this age group are more active in volunteer work than they have ever been. They bring their experience and professional skills to the volunteer organizations where they serve. Most of them say, "I've never been so busy, and I love it."

Recruiting the Retiring Professional

While retiring professionals love to volunteer, volunteer managers must still be careful when they recruit this new and growing 21st century resource. Here are three very important factors to remember.

Retiring professionals want to make a difference. Retiring professionals don't just want to make a contribution; they desire a significant role making a difference. These people were ready to change the world in the 1960s, and they still strongly believe in causes. So make sure that your mission is something that people can get excited about.

My wife, Susie—who will quickly point out that she is not yet 64—is an ESL (English as a second language) college professor teaching graduate students. I've been a speaker and trainer for more than 40 years, and we dream about volunteering to teach overseas. So the last thing we want to do is to stuff envelopes somewhere. We want to fulfill a dream!

Does that mean we're not interested in getting our hands dirty or doing labor? Not at all! We're not afraid of jumping in with a team when a job needs to get done. In fact, we've stuffed thousands of envelopes, set up hundreds of chairs and tables, cleaned dozens of bathrooms, and swept countless floors. However, the organization that uses high-quality, professionally trained volunteers only to do unskilled labor will lose many retiring professional volunteers. We want to be recruited to use a lifetime of experience to help you accomplish your vision. And we're not alone.

In fact, you might be thinking, "That sounds like what you said about the younger generation." Yes, members of the younger generation also want to use their professional skills to help accomplish your vision. The difference between the two is this: The younger generation will tell you up front that they don't want to stuff envelopes or other trivial tasks. Retiring professionals will probably accept the job, but they won't volunteer for you again.

JONATHAN
Wow! You "really old" people are passive-aggressive.

TOM I guess we could be like your generation—disrespectful.

JONATHAN Shut up! I mean, yes father, you're right. And truthfully, I gotta give you props for sticking it out for a day, even when you don't want to be there.

TOM Props?

JONATHAN Oh yeah—I forgot that I'm talking to someone who remembers what he was doing when Kennedy was shot. "Props" means credit or recognition. It's like, "Hey, Dad, props to you for making it through that movie without having to go to the bathroom!"

TOM "Fo' shizzle."

Now let's get back to retiring professionals.

Retiring professionals aren't afraid of commitment. Let's be more specific. This older generation of potential volunteers isn't afraid of commitment when there's a payoff. The payoff could be your cause, or a benefit to us.

A very popular volunteer program for retired professionals is the Master Gardener program offered by many communities. New Master Gardeners are required to contribute 50 hours of community volunteer work over 12 months. Every year thereafter, the program requires 25 hours of volunteer activity.

Each spring, volunteers attend a one-hour class each week for 15 weeks. Applicants must attend all 15 classes and pay a fee for materials. University specialists, horticulture advisors, and community experts teach the classes. Topics include introduction to horticulture, water and fertilizer management, planting and maintenance of trees, and so forth. After attending all the sessions, and after completing all the weekly quizzes and a final exam, trainees receive a graduation certificate. Retiring professionals willingly make the commitment to programs like Master Gardener because of the payoff. Part of the "what's in it for me" attitude remains relevant for Boomers, and they'll commit to training, study, dues, and even long-term obligations when they feel it's worth it.

Retiring professionals want flexibility. They're often on the go, so they appreciate flexibility. You might think this sounds like a contradiction, because the commitment of the Master Gardener program seems like a lot. It is at first—but after the 15 weeks, the program has a lot of flexibility. This just demonstrates that retired professionals are willing to pay their dues, but they want flexibility as part of the payoff, too.

Jim, a retired dentist, volunteers for the local chapter of the Rotary Club. He paints and cleans for an inner-city project because he really cares about the problems of the inner city. Yet at times, the Rotary Club won't see Jim for a long time, because he and his wife, Sue, travel about six months of the year.

When Jim and Sue are home, they spend a lot of time volunteering. Jim would never volunteer to be on a board that required regular meetings. But he loves projects. Last year, Jim and Sue spent six months working in an orphanage in Eastern Europe doing dental work and even some basic construction work.

Don't miss the opportunity to recruit retiring professionals. They want to make a difference, they aren't afraid of commitments, and they like flexibility.

The Young Professionals

JONATHAN How would you describe the leading edge of Gen Y— specifically, the part of this new generation of young professionals currently in their 20s? This includes people like LeBron James (born in 1984), Hilary Duff (born in 1987), and Lindsey Lohan (born in 1986). Are these 20-somethings a good source of volunteers?

Despite the sometimes-negative headlines generated by some of the more well-known members of this generation, most of what we're learning reveals that this younger generation is volunteering in mass numbers. According to data from the Corporation for National and Community Service, 11.6 million Millennials dedicated 1.2 billion hours of service to communities across the country in 2010, with 21.2 percent of Millennials volunteering that year.[19]

Generational researchers Neil Howe and William Strauss make some extremely optimistic predictions about the generation born after 1981, who they call Millennials. They make the prediction "that by the time the last Millennials come of age, they could become...the cleanest-cut young adults in living memory."[20] Howe and Strauss go on to say that this generation will also be known for its hard work "on a grassroots reconstruction of community, teamwork, and civic spirit. They're doing it in the realms of community service, race, gender relations, politics and faith." The researchers note that this generation will have a tremendous capacity to mobilize volunteers for worthwhile causes, largely by use of the Internet.[21]

You might be wondering, if all this is true, then where are they? If this generation is so great, why can't we get them to help us?

You might also be skeptical, wondering how predictive studies like these can even be valid. After all, Strauss and Howe began making their predictions about this generation back in 1991, when the oldest members of Gen Y were just 9 years old.

I understand some of your skepticism. Call me old-fashioned, but I don't give a lot of weight to statistics unless I also observe those conclusions firsthand. When it comes to Gen Y, I immediately meshed this data with what I've seen of this generation when speaking at school assemblies and events across the country. In addition, I decided to do a little research of my own. I tapped into my database of more than 16,000 youth workers who are now recruiting older members of Gen Y to work with teenagers. I polled a group of them, asking questions about this young generation's reliability, passion, attitude, and skills. I then compared my results with existing research (like Strauss and Howe), as well as my own personal observations.

When all was said and done, I came up with a number of qualities that you need to understand as a volunteer manager so you can recruit and manage Gen Y volunteers—volunteers who are willing and excited to help you make a difference. Let's take a look at these seven characteristics, as well as a *"So what?"* for each one that provides a few tips on harnessing the potential of this generation as volunteers.

1. They're impatient. "Googled" is a verb—as in "I Googled it"—that has replaced going to the library or the store. More than prior generations, this new group of young professionals shops online (often at 2 a.m.) and researches products on the Internet so they can be prepared and informed buyers. This generation grew up in the information age with everything available at the click of a button.

They grew up with video games, computers in the classrooms, and fast-paced television programming.

By playing video games, they learned that when you win, you're automatically promoted to the next level. So they're impatient to move up the organizational leadership chart. When this generation completes a task, they want to know, "Where's the next challenge?" or "When do I get to be in charge?"

So what? As a volunteer manager, give these young professionals an opportunity to use their gifts and abilities. If they perform well, give them a little more responsibility. Yes, they might be impatient, but be tolerant of this. Many of them really are quick learners. Look for the kernel of truth behind their impatience; you might expose some areas in your organization that need improvement.

2. They're multitaskers. Kaiser Family Foundation's 2010 report on media consumption by children—*Generation M2: Media in the Lives of 8- to 18-Year-Olds*—notes that today's seventh- through 12th-graders regularly consume two or more media concurrently. The Internet has opened the doors to many of these media sources with social networking sites, YouTube, and platforms like iTunes® with downloadable songs and videos.

Researchers suggest that this saturation of available media has morphed kids into media multitaskers. "Nearly one in three (31%) 8- to 18-year-olds say that 'most' of the time they are doing homework, they are also using one medium or another—watching TV, texting, listening to music, and so on."[22]

The Kaiser Foundation argues that we need to give our full attention to anything that takes up this much space in young people's lives. Here's what researchers noted in a previous report, from 2005:

This generation truly is the media generation, devoting more than a quarter of each day to media. As media devices become increasingly portable, and as they spread even further through young people's environments...media messages will become an even more ubiquitous presence in an already media-saturated world.[23]

Reports like these make note of multitasking in their statistics. When Kaiser reported that this generation averaged seven and a half hours per day of media consumption in 2010, researchers had to qualify the statement. A large percentage of these kids are actually exposed to the equivalent of 10 hours and 45 minutes of media content each day, even though they pack that into a little more than 7½ hours of time. In other words, it's not uncommon for kids to watch a DVD while listening to iTunes and checking their Facebook status.

I came face to face with this younger generation's skill for multitasking when I tried to battle my son at one of his new Xbox® games. Call me old, but I used to be pretty good with an Atari® joystick. It was easy—a stick and a button. Have you seen an Xbox control? It's like the front of a cockpit! We've come a long way from Pong. My son can work the all the buttons on the control with ease while I'm still trying to figure out how to get my character to walk without bumping into walls. He'll do a quick move and then tell me to do the same. "It's easy, Dad," he assures me. "Just move around the corner (with the left joystick), jump (using the A button), punch the 'Grunt' (B button), aim at the 'Elite' on the balcony (right joystick), throw a grenade (L trigger), and fire your SMG (R trigger) as you strafe sideways (left joystick again)." Of course, my son can do that in 2 microseconds while chewing gum and whistling to the music he's blasting.

So what? As a volunteer manager, be tolerant when this generation does things differently than "the way we've always done it." They might accomplish things faster and more efficiently (all while playing loud music). When possible, ask what they can offer to your mission.

Instead of just giving them a "to-do" list, ask them to help you achieve your desired outcomes.

3. They think "digital." Have you even tried to train a 23-year-old? They process data completely differently than retiring professionals do. If you're used to working with Baby Boomers, remember this: The retiring generation is analog. Young professionals are digital.

Retiring professionals think more like a videotape. If you don't like a part of a movie, you have to fast-forward. Gen Y has never had to fast-forward. They just jump to whatever chapter they want on their DVD. "Hey, skip through the beginning. Let's jump right to where Katniss begins her training!"

Sorry, Boomers and retiring professionals, members of Gen Y don't even like your outlines. A lot of retiring professionals think in points I, II, and III, maybe with some neat little A, B, and C subpoints. But members of this younger generation aren't bound by such linear structure. They can jump to the last chapter without a fast-forward. They process information quickly and embrace change. They don't sit around and wait for things to happen when they know they can make things happen.

Marc Prensky, a pioneer of digital game-based learning and CEO and founder of games2train.com, coined the term "Twitch Speed." He says that this generation thinks and operates at higher speeds than previous generations. They grew up on video games, MTV (more than 100 images a minute), and quick-cut action films. If you want to see what Prensky is talking about, watch five minutes of the newest *CSI*, and then watch a rerun of *Magnum P.I.* You'll be surprised at how slow *Magnum P.I.* has become in its old age.

Marc makes this contention: "The under-30 generation has had far more experience of processing information quickly than its predecessors, and is therefore better at it."[24] Companies or organizations that hire members of this digital generation often make the mistake of boring them to death in a training class taught by a terrible communicator, or forcing them to watch slow, outdated, anesthetizing training videos.

So what? As a volunteer manager, provide opportunities for young professionals to make an impact and to see the difference they're making. They don't want to wait for someone else to make a difference—they want to do it. Give them that opportunity and they'll begin to grow roots in your organization.

And don't bore these potential volunteers right out of your training room. Use training as an opportunity to motivate and inspire your volunteers for your cause. Like no other generation before them, this younger generation is cause-driven. Hire a dynamic and cutting-edge trainer to capture the hearts of these volunteers and motivate them to make a difference. (I probably do about a dozen of these types of trainings each year for youth ministry organizations around the country, engaging these young workers with a lot of media and relevant examples from youth culture.)

4. They're tolerant. I probably don't have to tell you that this younger generation is growing up in a much more integrated world than even Gen Xers. Gen Y is growing up with friends and heroes of all types. Diversity is a value for this generation. They display an incredible tolerance and a slowness to judge other people.

You might be thinking, "What? These young people are rude and outspoken!" Valid observation, but don't confuse that with being judgmental. Young professionals have a great spirit of openness. True products of the civil rights movement, these young people don't display the same prejudices that divided earlier generations. They're great team members, ignoring gender and racial biases to work with anyone to accomplish common goals. My friend Lane Palmer from Dare 2 Share agrees with this assessment in an article he wrote about this generation posted on Ypulse.com (one of the best Internet resources providing insight about Gen Y). Lane says:

Much like the young people of the 1960s, these adolescents do not have an inherent respect for titles and/or positions. Yet unlike the Woodstock folks, they generally aren't actively anti-establishment. What registers with them is personal authenticity and passion about life regardless of background, education, or societal "rank." [25]

So what? As a volunteer manager, make sure you practice diversity (ethnic, gender, generational) in recruiting, promoting, and hiring leadership. Most of this young generation ignores biases and works with anyone who can help them accomplish common goals.

Provide opportunities for members of this young generation to get to know each other and bond together with your entire team of workers. If you give them opportunities to grow as a team, they'll be great team players. Provide fun annual training retreats where they can connect together. Use team-building games and activities regularly in your meetings.

For team-building activities, see page 264.

If you capture the respect of this young generation, they might easily prove to be your most valuable volunteers. Nearly all the youth and children's workers I surveyed noted how committed members of this young generation were to their teams.

5. They're looking for causes. Although this is true of most volunteers across generational lines, this young generation is highly motivated by causes. They're always looking for ways to make a difference and to make their mark. Volunteering can provide that. When the match is right, they're highly committed and fiercely loyal.

Regina Blink, volunteer coordinator for the Society of the Blind in Sacramento, raved about Stacey, a high school student who called her and asked if she could do graphic arts work for the organization as a school project. Regina emailed her the information and Stacey developed a professional design for one project. The people at the Society of the Blind were thrilled, and that project extended into a two-year volunteer relationship between Stacey and the organization.

Members of Gen Y, like the Boomers of the '60s, want to make a difference. Many young professionals are putting the pressure on their employers to be socially responsible. Seventy percent of 18- to 26-year-olds polled in a 2011 Deloitte Volunteer IMPACT survey said they would prefer to work for a company with a strong community to its community—and even among individuals who said they rarely or never volunteer, that figure was strong, at 61 percent.[26]

So what? As a volunteer manager, devote considerable time to communicating your cause to your young volunteers. In training sessions, don't just teach process; teach desired outcomes. Once they're convinced of your cause, these volunteers will seek out ways to make a difference for your organization.

Also, provide community service opportunities. This generation might come to you at first because they "have to" for a school project or required community service hours. But if you inspire them, making your passion their passion, you'll make incredible allies.

6. They're team players, but... In Chapter 1, we talked about the seismic shift of isolation. We painted the picture of today's young people alone in their house, but on the computer with hundreds of e-friends. Isolated, yet surrounded.

To review this information, go back to "Seismic Shift 2—Isolation: From Community to Individualism."

This young generation is often a living contradiction. They're a generation of loners that make for great team players. They love to seclude themselves with video games and iPods, but their favorite activity is to just "hang out" together.

In my survey about this generation, one youth minister said, "I had big-time 'hang-out' people. I would sometimes need to fake a death scene for them to get the hint about leaving my house!"

Most volunteer managers that I've talked to seem to agree that this young generation loves opportunities to build "community." Maybe it's due to the fact that people have fewer close friends today than most people had a decade ago. Maybe they're trying to fill an interpersonal void in their life that e-friends just don't fill. Whatever the reason, they seem to be seeking community. And they seem to realize that volunteering might provide opportunities to build new relationships. Cash in on this opportunity.

A desire to "hang out" doesn't automatically mean "team player." Is this generation truly filled with team players or loners? My take is that many members of this generation want to be a part of a *winning team*—a team that makes a difference.

However, there is a *but*. They want to be a unique part of the team. They want to be able to use their gifts and abilities to make a difference. How many times have you heard, "There's no 'I' in 'team' "? Well, this younger generation might tell you that there *is* an "I" in "win."

Chap Clark, associate professor of youth, family, and culture at Fuller Seminary, presents another interesting perspective in his insightful book *Hurt: Inside the World of Today's Teenagers*. Clark contends that today's middle adolescents (ages 15-18) have been abandoned by a society that has moved from a "relatively stable and cohesive community intent on caring for the needs of the young, to a free-for-all of independent and fragmented adults seeking their own survival." So today's teenagers have found themselves in a "deepening hole of systematic rejection," which Clark calls "abandonment."[27]

Because of feeling abandoned and rejected, these young people seek a safe place in their smaller groups of friends that Clark calls "clusters."[28] But their desire for community doesn't stop with their own age group. Clark found that contrary to popular opinion, middle adolescents want significant relationships with adults as well, if adults are willing to trust them.[29]

What I found interesting is that I did my research for the first edition of this book in 2007. Clark added to his extensive research by serving as substitute high school teacher while on sabbatical in the 2001-2002 academic year.[30] The 16-year-old high school students of 2001 are now in the life stage that we're focusing on—the young professionals of 2012. And although Clark focuses mostly on high school students, he notes that as middle adolescents mature and leave home for college or military service, they seem to have a willingness to explore new relationships.[31] They move beyond their "clusters" and look for new groups. In my own experience, this group loves to cluster with people who share a similar mission or cause. And they still seek relationships with caring, older adults who will trust them.

So what? As a volunteer manager, make sure that you provide opportunities for these young professionals to get to know each other and bond together with your entire team of workers. Nine out of 10 Gen Y workers say they would like their workplace to be "social and fun."[32] These young adults want community both with people their own age and with adults who trust them, so take the opportunity to provide both of these needs. However, you must also be willing to empower members of this generation and give them opportunities to share their insights and skills. This gives you an opportunity to win their trust as you provide a safe place of acceptance and service.

7. They don't want to be managed; they want to be led. One of the best-run camping programs I've observed is Camp Timber-lee in East Troy, Wisconsin. I speak there several times a year and I'm always amazed at the quality volunteers who work at the camp. I asked Chris Radloff, the camp's director of youth programs, for his take on working with young volunteers. Chris told me this:

They don't want to be managed; they want to be led. By the time I have my staff for a few weeks, I don't need to give them commands. If I said, "I don't want you to leave the property," they'd respond, "Forget you... you can't stop me!" Instead I let them know, "My preference is that you don't leave the property tonight." By this time I've earned their respect. I've never had someone leave.

Chris states his *preference* and his volunteers abide by it because they respect his leadership.

So what? As a volunteer manager, be careful not to micromanage this younger generation. Help them understand your mission, your cause, and your desired outcomes. Earn their respect. As you earn their trust and get them excited about your cause, they'll follow your lead.

👆 *For more on helping volunteers understand your mission, earning their respect, and getting them excited, go to "Chapter 9: Leading the Successful Volunteer Organization."*

Quick Review

We've covered a lot of ground in this chapter about two groups that make up part of the new breed of volunteers. So let's review.

Recruiting and managing retiring professionals. How can you recruit and manage the whole new group of retiring professionals who are willing and excited to help you make a difference? Ask these questions about yourself and your organization to see if you're really "retiring professional"-friendly:

- Do you have a cause? Retiring professionals want to make a difference, not a contribution.

- Are you providing opportunities for retiring professionals to use their professional skills?

- Are you keeping the standard high? Retiring Boomers don't want to work alongside half-committed, unprofessional, "any old way will do" volunteers.

- Are you highlighting the payoffs? Make sure volunteers know what's in it for them, as well as how their work benefits your cause or mission.

- Are you providing flexibility? These volunteers are on the go and will often volunteer for more than one organization.

Recruiting and managing young professionals. How can you recruit and manage the whole new group of young volunteers who are willing and excited to help you make a difference? Ask these questions about yourself and your organization to see if you're really "young professional"-friendly:

- Are you mission-driven? Don't tell members of this young generation, "Please do this job and have it done by Friday." Instead, say, "What can you do to help us accomplish our mission?" Get to know them as individuals and listen to their input.

- Are you a coach to these young individuals? Be a coach—not a traditional manager. A coach challenges volunteers to do their best, yet nurtures individuals and encourages them to reach their full potential.

- Do you involve this young generation in decision-making? They want to be a part of the team in making decisions.

- Does your group practice diversity (ethnic, gender, generational) in recruiting, promoting, hiring, and seeking leadership? This young generation ignores gender and racial biases and works with anyone who can help them accomplish common goals.

- Do you take advantage of the community service requirements that many schools require? This young generation puts in hundreds of hours of volunteering by the time they graduate from high school and/or college. Do you have opportunities where they can be inspired by your organization, not just serve?

THE VOLUNTEER
MANAGER

As you step into your role as a volunteer manager, you need to understand how to empower the new breed of volunteer, who wants to be led, not managed. "Manager" is the position, not the method. "Coaching" is the work of the manager.

Chapter 5: Motivating the New Breed of Volunteers
Retain Volunteers by Motivating Them

Chapter 6: Empowering Volunteers to Do It Their Way
Move From Delegation to Empowerment

Chapter 7: Using a New Breed of Technology
Social Media, Wikis, Texting…and the Virtual Volunteer

Chapter 8: Managing or Canning High-Maintenance Volunteers
Performance Coaching the Volunteer From Hell

MOTIVATING THE NEW BREED OF VOLUNTEERS

Retain Volunteers by Motivating Them

It's a good thing Travis is a strong recruiter, because he has a problem retaining volunteers at the community parks volunteer organization he leads. Although he follows all the recruiting practices we discussed in Chapters 1 to 4, he just can't seem to retain his volunteers. His turnover rate is terrible.

He told us, "I need help managing my volunteers. I just can't seem to get them to do what I thought they were going to do when I recruited them."

Travis doesn't need help being a volunteer recruiter; he needs help being a volunteer manager. He needs to learn how to manage his volunteers once he gets them. And that's what Chapters 5 to 8 are all about.

Some people in the volunteer world really don't like the word *manager*. When we think of managing, we think of stuff. We manage materials. But today's volunteers are savvy "knowledge workers" who don't want to be treated like stuff. They want to be empowered. They want to be coached. They want to be led.

While we like "coach" as a title, the reality is that many of us bear the title "volunteer manager." Here's our take on it: "Manager" is the position, not the method. "Coaching" is the work of the manager. So we'll keep referring to volunteer managers, knowing that coaching is what they do.

These managers don't just give orders. They nurture and lead because they know how to empower people to use their gifts, talents, passion, and ideas to accomplish the mission of the organization.

So how do we get volunteers to do what we want and need them to do in the 21st century? What's going to motivate them to stick around?

Obviously not the pay!

TOM I was serving on a search committee for an organization and getting discouraged that the process was taking much too long. I almost felt as if I wasn't a good fit on the committee, and wondered if the committee would get along better without me.

While out of town on business during one of the committee's weekly meetings and flying back home, I drafted a letter of resignation. I planned to send it to other committee members the next day. But when I got home, I was surprised to find the following short note in the mail:

Dear Tom,

We really missed you at our last meeting. I appreciate your input into our discussions and how much we all depend on your expertise.

Thanks,
Stephen (Chairman)

I didn't send my letter of resignation.

JONATHAN **TOM** You might call motivation an inside job. Volunteers do things for their own reasons, not yours, so your role is to create an organizational culture that stimulates the inner motivation of each volunteer. What can you do from the outside to arouse that inner motivation?

The following motivation and retention tips are winners. We've provided you with a baker's dozen. Follow these 13 essentials and you'll create a culture that motivates the new breed of volunteer.

1. Discover What Motivates Volunteers

Why do people join your organization? What motivates them to invest time, money, and talent and become involved in any organization or ministry? And what does it take to get them to stay involved?

Answer these questions, and you'll tap into the motivational drives of the new breed of volunteer. Once you tap into what motivates them to volunteer, you can also tap into what motivates them to stick around. Let's explore this briefly.

Most people respond to the following three levels of motivation:

The self-serving motivational drive. People join an organization because it meets their needs. This need might be for business, friendship, belonging, or many other self-serving needs. And they stay because an organization continues to meet those needs. When a volunteer makes a commitment to work in your organization, tap into that self-serving inner motivation.

The relational drive. People also commit because of friendship. When a friend personally asks, most people have a hard time saying no. A friend excited about your organization's cause is the best person to recruit. Investing in relationships can be one of the strongest stimulators when it comes to motivating volunteers.

The core motivational drive—their beliefs. For most volunteers, their core motivational drive—what they believe in—represents the strongest level of commitment. This takes place when volunteers commit to your organization because of their passion—meaning that they actually believe in your cause. Even if this cause will cost them a great deal of personal sacrifice and pain, these volunteers remain highly motivated. Ghandi and Mother Teresa weren't motivated by self-serving drives or because of friends. They believed in their causes. People join and commit because they believe a cause is right. This is the highest level of motivation.

Your volunteers might initially join for one of the first two levels (self-serving or relational). But after they get a taste of what your organization does, they could become believers in your cause. Even if they start helping just to fulfill a community service requirement, they might—in time—become true believers and grow passionate about your cause. In fact, this should be your goal with all of your volunteers.

2. Give Regular Feedback

Sometimes when we lead volunteer manager training, we'll have participants play the feedback game. This training game can be humorous, but it's also very effective.

Participants line up on an imaginary line in the training room. One end of the line is January 1 and the other end of the line December 31. The participants get out of their seats (this works great when you have a group of about 20-30) and line up according to the day and month of their birthday in relationship to everyone else in the room. However, they can't communicate to each other about their birthdays. No talking, no hand signals, no blinking Morse code, nothing. They can only guess where they think they *should* stand.

Those with January birthdays immediately go to one end and the December birthdays the other. But everyone else has to figure where they stand. After a few frustrating minutes of trying to figure out where to stand on the line, they can then start speaking to each other to find their proper place. Most of the time, more than half the people need to change places.

When they've taken their spots, with everyone standing in the proper place, we say: "If you forget everything else we say today—don't forget this. This one statement can change how you coach and motivate people: Without feedback you don't know where you stand."

Steve served on the personnel committee of his church because of his background in human resources. His pastor asked him to write a report on state labor laws and other human-resource issues for the committee. Steve slaved over the report for a week, doing intensive research, writing and rewriting, and giving it to several people to proof. The report ended up being about 15 pages.

Finally the day arrived when the report was due. It was one of many pieces of paper handed in at the meeting. Steve figured that the pastor would at least mention it. But nothing.

Steve brought the report to the next meeting, thinking it would at least be on the agenda to address quickly.

Nothing again. He never heard anything about the report.

Several months later he finally asked the pastor if he'd received the report. After all, maybe it got lost in the paper shuffle. But his pastor replied, "Oh yeah. It was a great report." He even went on to detail particular aspects of the report that were very helpful.

That's what Steve needed.

Steve didn't need praise. He didn't need his ego stroked. He just wanted to hear if what he worked on had been helpful. He wanted some consolation that his 20 hours of work was worth it—that he was making a difference.

People want to make a difference. Without feedback, they don't know if they're making a difference.

Have you ever coached a sports team like Little League or soccer? If so, you know that you can't wait until the rewards banquet to give feedback. You have to provide feedback every day, all the time. It's essential for great coaching. And it's essential for great volunteer management.

Personal *thank you* notes are a simple but effective way to give feedback. At the California State Railroad Museum, all paid supervisors keep thank you cards or stationery in their desks. They each make a daily habit of catching a volunteer doing something good and dropping that person a quick note of specific thanks.

When he was chief curator at the museum Stephen Drew personally wrote two letters a day based on the database. No wonder this organization's volunteer retention rate is very high. Brandi Barris, volunteer coordinator at the museum since early 2011, said that in 2011, they had an average 90 percent retention rate from the 71 people who graduated from a 56-hour training class. In other words, 90 percent of the 71 people kept their commitment through the following year. Brandy said that they are very intention about keeping in touch with their 600 volunteers by email—which is a huge job— and it is paying off. By the way, thank you notes have a generational twist. Gen Y volunteers won't even notice the difference between a letter, an email, or a text. In fact, volunteer managers will find that if they ask Gen Y volunteers about a letter they sent, the volunteers will respond, "Oh, I didn't see that. Just send me a text next time." Many Boomers and other retiring professionals are the exact opposite. They'll appreciate that you took the time to actually handwrite a note.

👆 *To review the similarities and differences between these two generations of potential volunteers, go back to "Chapter 4: Tapping Into Two New Breeds of Volunteers."*

It's crucial that you provide regular and frequent feedback. Your volunteers need encouragement, thank you's, and even a little constructive criticism at times.

MEASURE YOUR FEEDBACK

How are you at giving feedback? Do you want to know?
Measure your feedback.

Try the following assignment for one month.

- Write down each volunteer that you supervise.

- By each person's name, write down the number of
  tasks he or she does in a month (for example, 50).

- Write down the number of times each week you
  recognize each person for that task (for example, 2).

- Subtract the second number (2) from the first number
  (50) = 48.

- Try to close the gap.

For some ideas about increasing the feedback you give volunteers,
go to "8. Provide Tangible Incentives" in this section.

Without feedback volunteers don't know where they stand.

3. Offer Special Privileges and Perks

Volunteers love perks. As a volunteer manager, it's this simple for
you: Perks help retention.

The California State Railroad Museum in Old Sacramento has been
using volunteers successfully since it opened in 1981. Its excellent
volunteer program includes many perks and privileges. The program
currently has more than 600 volunteers, and over 400 of those

qualified for an appreciation banquet for people who volunteered at least one hour a week for a whole year.

Docents (tour guides) at the museum receive a complimentary annual membership that entitles them to a discount in the museum store, a quarterly newsletter, invitations to exhibit openings, and behind-the-scenes events. For those who work their way up the ranks of the museum's volunteer chain, the ultimate perk is being able to drive an authentic steam engine. This might sound like small potatoes, but for people who love trains, it's huge.

JONATHAN One of the best perks I've discovered for youth ministry volunteers is pretty simple: Just don't make them spend their own money.

When Lori and I were first married, we volunteered at a local church helping with the high school group. The youth pastor wanted all his volunteers to attend retreats and camps with the group, but he asked us to pay our own way. Lori and I were dirt-poor back then. I was going to school and working part time. Lori was earning a little, too. But let me put it this way: Taco Bell was a real treat! So $100 here and $150 there was not just a stretch, it was impossible. To make matters worse, we paid a $30 fee to be fingerprinted and another $15 or $20 occasionally for our small group curriculum. Needless to say, we were a little apprehensive about signing up the next year.

When I became a full-time youth worker, I vowed not to do this to my volunteers. I learned to budget events so volunteer staff could attend for free. Here's an easy example: If you take all your students to a place that costs $8, charge $10 or $12 to cover gas and admission of your volunteers. Most students that can come up with 8 bucks can come up with a few more. This just takes a little planning. However, the payoff is huge! You communicate to your volunteers how much you appreciate their time and dedication.

I not only paid for these volunteers to attend events, I also gave them perks. Often this involved simply rewarding them for the stuff I wanted them to do. For example, on weeklong trips, one primary goal was for volunteers to spend one-on-one time with students. So every morning, I gave each volunteer an envelope with $5 in it. I told them to find a time that day to take out a student for a shake or french fries and a soda. I remember a trip where I had eight volunteers on a six-day trip. That's 48 envelopes with $5 in each, for a total of $240. Sound like a lot? Well that $240 guaranteed that 48 students received one-on-one attention from an adult for about a half-hour. That's more than a lot of them got at home in a week. Best $240 I ever spent. I just put it in the budget for the trip.

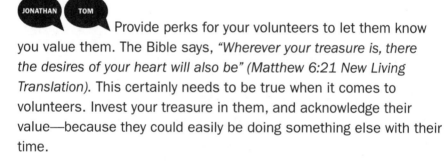 Provide perks for your volunteers to let them know you value them. The Bible says, *"Wherever your treasure is, there the desires of your heart will also be" (Matthew 6:21 New Living Translation).* This certainly needs to be true when it comes to volunteers. Invest your treasure in them, and acknowledge their value—because they could easily be doing something else with their time.

4. Send Volunteers to Conferences

Any volunteer manager knows that volunteer training is essential. But how can you motivate your volunteers to attend?

Many people who serve as volunteers feel that they already know how to do their jobs. For example, you might have a successful business manager volunteer. Often, people who lead effective businesses think that they're prepared and trained to lead volunteer teams. However, coaching volunteers is very different from managing employees. You can face a hard job trying to teach people who feel that they already know what do to. So how can you motivate them to learn?

One way is by putting money in your budget to send leaders to conferences. Most conferences are at resort towns and offer a getaway. These events are filled with activities and helpful seminars for volunteer leaders. People leave "pumped" and filled with ideas. And they network and exchange ideas with other volunteers who struggle with some of the same issues.

These conferences offer two benefits: training and motivation.

TOM The American Society of Association Executives and its state chapters offer continual training. As a regular trainer for these conferences, I see volunteer board members who are challenged and encouraged as we work together. The California Travel Parks Association sends its president to the CalSAE (California Society of Association Executives) training sessions. I talked with their president after he attended one of these sessions, and he was energized. He told me, "It was so helpful to talk with presidents of other associations and exchange ideas. I felt that I wasn't the alone. Other leaders had the same questions that I had."

JONATHAN If you're in youth ministry, you can take your volunteers to national conferences offered by organizations like Group Publishing and Youth Specialties. I teach at conferences like these every year and interact with hundreds of volunteers. These volunteers love the fun and fellowship that the conferences provide, in addition to what they learn.

Of course, by the time you pay for travel, hotel, and meal expenses, these conferences might be a little too expensive for small churches or youth ministry organizations. No worries. Group, Youth Specialties, and the ministry I lead—The Source for Youth Ministry—all offer affordable Saturday training events in cities across the U.S. These provide a great opportunity to travel with your volunteers for just a day to learn together.

I tried to make it a priority to take youth volunteers to either of these types of training conferences at least once a year.

JONATHAN TOM Do your best to send your volunteer leaders to conferences that fit your organization. They'll come back with a new passion and vision for your organization's mission.

5. Provide On-the-Job Vocational Training

Have you ever considered offering vocational training for volunteers as a way to retain them? For example, you could target stay-at-home moms who are sending children off to college—women who might be looking to update their work skills. Even in the 21st century, a good number of moms stay at home and have time available during the day while their kids are in school. Many of these moms are college graduates or have work experience, but they haven't worked for 5 to 10 years. Your organization could greatly benefit from these volunteers while offering them some updated skill training at the same time.

TOM I worked for an organization where we recruited 20 women to volunteer four hours a week in our office. We had the latest computer equipment (this was 1984, when the PC was becoming popular). We trained these women to use the newest software, and they committed to volunteering for us. We sent them to classes and trained them on the job.

It doesn't take a genius to figure out that 4 hours times 20 women equaled 80 hours of work a week.

JONATHAN Hold on. I'm getting my calculator…

TOM *Sigh.* Eighty hours is the equivalent of two full-time employees. With the money we saved on wages, we purchased the latest office equipment. Each woman committed for a year, but most of them worked for three or four years because they loved volunteering for our organization.

As a benefit to them, they were able to update their résumés and find part-time and full-time jobs as their children went off to college. Talk about a win/win.

JONATHAN **TOM** Student interns can provide a similar source of volunteers. Some students might work for your organization to add the experience to their résumé. Other students get college credit. But many of them will volunteer as interns because they really want practical experience working in the field your organization represents. These make the best kind of volunteers, because they not only achieve work experience, they also enjoy the field and cause of your organization. This means they're motivated at that core level—the belief level.

Providing vocational training for volunteers will affect your organization in a positive way even if volunteers leave after the requested commitment period. But often, training and development activities inspire volunteers to stick around far longer because you've given them additional reasons to love and appreciate your organization.

6. Be Available to Volunteers

Whether it's the Girl Scouts, hospital staff, or local churches, we hear this one all the time from the paid staff of organizations: "The volunteers want to sit around and visit, but we've got so much work to do." Often, volunteers do expect to spend time visiting with the paid staff, both as a way to learn more about the organization and sometimes just to socialize. Often, the paid staff gets frustrated with the interruptions.

TOM One drawback to our 20 office volunteers was the time many of them wanted to spend visiting with our staff. They felt that one of the perks of volunteering included time with the staff to find out what was happening in the organization. At first I resented this, but I soon realized that we needed to spend time with them. After all, they were doing work that represented the organization's cause and mission.

We began to invite them to coffee times during breaks. We spent time interacting with them, asking them about their families. Then, as we walked with them back to their workstations, we took a few minutes to comment on their work and how much we appreciated it. We made a point of being very specific. For example, I'd say something like, "Connie, thanks so much for the report you prepared for me last week. I used the information you provided to write an article for our national publication. When the article comes out next month, I'll be sure you get a copy." And when the article was published, I sent Connie a copy with a handwritten message across the top of the page saying, "I couldn't have written this without your help."

JONATHAN **TOM** So what can you do to be available to your volunteers? Even if it's just during a coffee break, create an arena where volunteers have a little time to chat. If not, they'll probably do it anyway—during a time you need them to do something else. Giving your volunteers this time not only gives you interaction with them, it also gives them time with each other. Although this might seem trivial to you, it might mean the world to them.

7. Provide Free Food

What is it about food that motivates people? One summer we led management workshops in five locations of a government agency. The overall supervisor was concerned about the lack of motivation in these offices, and her concerns were founded. After spending a few days in each branch office, we discovered that four of the offices were relatively dead, but one was alive. The difference? Food!

In this particular office, the 30 employees took turns bringing in bagels, donuts, or home-baked goodies on Wednesday morning. When you count holidays, each employee only had to bring in treats once every 35 weeks. Out of 52 weeks a year, that isn't bad. On each Wednesday morning, the employees in this office spent time in the break room laughing, sharing stories, and enjoying a wonderful time of interaction. The "opening exercises" of work—the rituals that happen every day in every workplace when people get ready to start work—took a little bit longer on Wednesdays. But the payoff was amazing.

When we mentioned this idea to the other four offices, we received great resistance. People made all kinds of jokes about "that party office." But in reality "that party office" was the top-producing office.

The point is that what's true for paid staff might be even more important for your volunteers. Offer free snacks for your volunteers to motivate and encourage them. Bring bagels, donuts, or fruit to a volunteer meeting, or have sandwiches delivered to a long evening meeting.

 My wife, Susie, and I put on a special Christmas luncheon at our home every year for those 20 office volunteers I mentioned earlier. We simply included the cost of the luncheon in our volunteer budget, and our paid office staff prepared and served the food. This was a special time, and we always had 100 percent turnout.

The children's director at our church had one of the greatest turnouts for training that we've ever seen. When we asked what her secret was, she said, "Good food."

She wasn't kidding. One of her volunteers was a chef at a local restaurant. He offered to cater every one of her quarterly trainings for several hundred teachers. We're not talking burgers and hot dogs. This guy served the most incredible gourmet dishes. Plenty of food and it was free. Needless to say, this children's director had booming attendance.

Our friend Rob has a bunch of young Generation Y volunteers. He quickly discovered the power of food as a motivator. In our survey of volunteer leaders, Rob wrote this:

I've given my volunteers a reason to get to events early. I feed them! For the past year my wife and I have cooked an awesome meal each Monday night. Four to six of our volunteers—all aged 20-26—come and claim it's the best meal of the week. We really do feed them well and sit down as a family. My own boys (10 and 12) love it. I think this communicates that we really value each volunteer as a person and not just what he or she does for the program. Similarly, I took five volunteers to an event in Grass Valley and I treated them at Sizzler® on the way. You would have thought I bought them a new car!

Food can definitely be a great motivator. So use it to help retain your volunteers.

8. Provide Tangible Incentives

As volunteer managers, it's easy to think that because we're dealing with volunteers and they have a passion for our cause, they really don't want any tangible incentives. Guess again.

The following examples really do help motivate and retain volunteers:

Logo apparel. Provide all volunteers with top-quality shirts, sweaters, T-shirts, sweatshirts, or caps to wear when they volunteer. Don't scrimp! This provides a uniform, professional look, and most volunteers will wear their apparel in public—advertising your mission. One caution: Make sure that only volunteers get the apparel. Make what you give them special. In other words, if you sell clothing as a fundraiser, make it different from the items you give to your volunteers.

Restaurant gift certificates. Gift certificates for special recognition always score. These don't have to be to the most expensive restaurant in town (although that's nice). A $5 or $10 Starbucks® or Ben & Jerry's® gift card to all your volunteers will help them feel appreciated. Sometimes, businesses might even donate small gift certificates to your organization, because they know that when the people come to cash them in, they often spend more.

Say it with flowers. If you send flowers to a hospital or funeral, it's because you care. On Valentine's Day, you might send flowers to say, "I love you." We knew a couple who received two dozen red roses from the salesman who sold them a new Lexus® . The salesman was saying, "Thanks for my big commission." Bottom line: Flowers express a multitude of feelings and always represent a thoughtful expression of love and appreciation.

In addition, you can use very simple incentives like these:

- Personal awards given at meetings

- Write-ups in the organization newsletter

- Recognition plaques

9. Have Fun

Fun is an amazing motivator. Volunteer work can be stressful, but fun can serve as your most effective stress buster. Groups that play ball together, golf together, take a hike together, or even just have pizza together (food again), stay together.

Sometimes, passionate leaders of organizations that use volunteers have one drawback. These leaders—who are passionate about their cause—forget to laugh. Don't become so serious about your cause and your mission that you forget to have fun.

TOM I'll admit, this is an area of leadership that I struggled with. I often became so involved in the daily running of an organization—meeting payroll, paying bills, meeting the expectations of members, and managing employees—that I had trouble lightening up.

JONATHAN I can vouch for that.

TOM Of course, we haven't even mentioned the kind of leader who jokes too much!

JONATHAN Don't even go there.

 JONATHAN **TOM** How can you have fun when you have so much work to do? Something as simple as an employee or volunteer lounge can be a great stress buster. You can laugh and share time with volunteers before you return to your office.

Most volunteers, even if they already have a passion for your organization's mission, prefer to volunteer in a fun environment where they can enjoy their assignments and co-workers. A fun environment also includes specific celebrations for appreciation.

In fact, if you can reward volunteers and have fun in the process, you'll satisfy two important motivational drives: Volunteers get to enjoy their tasks, and they feel appreciated for the work they do.

10. Accountability

Last month, we chatted with a volunteer fireman who told us that his participation in the volunteer fire department totally dropped when the fire chief made a decision that backfired.

The fire chief always posted a list of volunteers with the number of calls they responded to each month. The fire chief decided that the chart was a waste of time, so he stopped posting it. Our friend told us that he lost count of the calls he responded to, and when he heard the fire alarm, he started choosing not to go. He thought, "I'll go next time."

After a few months, the fire chief recognized his mistake. Most of the volunteers told him that if they saw on the chart that the numbers of calls they responded to had fallen off, it motivated them to bring their numbers up. The fire chief reinstated the list and the numbers went up immediately.

Accountability, and even a little competition, isn't a bad thing. Without it, your volunteers might think they're doing more than they actually are.

11. Positive Gossip

When someone praises one of your volunteers, tell that volunteer about it. Secondhand compliments almost seem to get more reinforcement value than when you praise volunteers yourself.

TOM Gary, the director of social services in a California county, attends one of my leadership workshops on a regular basis. So I know him fairly well. One of his business colleagues told me how much she appreciated Gary's leadership. Then she said, "Wow, I don't know how Gary does it. He not only puts in hours at work in a very stressful job, but he's so involved in our Rotary community projects. Gary is a leader who I really respect, and we all know that he'll never let us down."

The next week I saw Gary at the workshop I was leading. My first words to him were, "Hey, we were just talking about you last week."

Then I told Gary what this colleague said about him. I think it made his day.

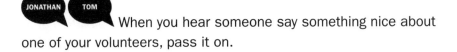 When you hear someone say something nice about one of your volunteers, pass it on.

12. Huddles

Wouldn't it be nice to have a quick meeting without it being a "meeting"? That's what a huddle is. Picture everyone gathering quickly in the morning for a quick overview of the day. People don't even need to sit down.

TOM I was giving a leadership workshop for the directors and teachers at Spectrum, a school for children with learning disabilities. Before my training session, the president of the school led a quick "morning huddle" to make some announcements. He announced that the school had received its updated accreditation. But what everyone remembered most was his recognition of one director who put in numerous volunteer hours compiling all of the information needed for the reaccreditation application. When the president read off all that she'd done, everyone stood and applauded for several minutes. Most of us felt overwhelmed at the hours she'd put in.

Then the school's president handed her two tickets to a performance of *Les Miserables* in San Francisco.

JONATHAN TOM Use a huddle to go over assignments, update communication, introduce new volunteers, and most important, take the opportunity to recognize a specific action of a volunteer. Be very specific! For example,

I want to say thank you to Matt for his work yesterday. He came in early and put together all of our packets for our session today. That is so Matt. Thanks a bunch for all you do to help us help the children of this community.

13. Thanking Families of Volunteers

This is a no-brainer. It's as simple as writing a note to the family members of a volunteer thanking them for their support of the volunteer. Acknowledge the good work their family member has done, and specifically explain that individual's importance to accomplishing the mission of your organization.

The Common Thread of Motivation

So what's common among these 13 motivational tools? The common thread is personal recognition and respect.

Thomas J. Watson Jr., former CEO of IBM, said this: "Our early emphasis on human relations was not motivated by altruism, but by the simple belief that if we respected our people and helped them respect themselves the company would make the most profit."[33]

If simple respect and thanks works for IBM, these simple but sincere methods of motivation can definitely work for your organization.

SELF CHECK-UP

Rate yourself regarding each of the following motivational practices.

4 = all of the time

3 = most of the time

2 = occasionally

1 = never

____ Tapping into the volunteer's motivational drives

____ Giving regular feedback

____ Giving regular rewards and recognition

____ Offering special privileges or incentives

____ Sending volunteers to conferences

____ Providing on-the-job vocational training

____ Being available to volunteers

____ Providing free food

____ Giving public affirmations

____ Having fun

____ Positive gossip

____ Huddles

____ Thanking families of volunteers

CHAPTER 6

EMPOWERING VOLUNTEERS TO DO IT THEIR WAY

Move From Delegation to Empowerment

In his book *A Passion for Excellence*, Tom Peters tells of an experiment where people in group "A" received puzzles to solve and some rather dull proofreading to do. While they did these two tasks, an audiotape played in the background; the sound included a person speaking Spanish, two people speaking Armenian, a mimeograph machine running, a chattering typewriter, and some street noise.

Another group, group "B," received the same projects and listened to the same tape. However, they also received a button they could push to suppress the noise. The group with the buttons to push solved five times as many puzzles and made just one-fourth of the proofreading errors as those who had no button.

Sure, you might be thinking, it was all that stinking noise!

Guess again. Amazingly, those who could push the button never pushed it once! The mere fact that they *could* push the button made the difference. They possessed the power of ownership.

Peters also tells how Ford Motor Co. executives revolutionized their Edison, New Jersey, plant when they made a gutsy move and gave the assembly line employees a button they could push to stop the line. Employees did use the buttons. "To be precise, they shut the facility down 20-30 times a day."[34] But each shutdown was only about 10 seconds. Although the stoppage was hardly noticeable, the quality improved as employees took ownership of the production. Peters says:

The number of defects per car produced dropped during the first month of the experiment from 17.2 per car to 0.8 per car. The number of cars requiring rework after they had come off the line fell by 97%. And the backlog of union grievances at any point in the facility plummeted from an average of well over 200 to an average of less than 12.[35]

But Peters adds that what was far more significant than the turnaround in quality was the change in attitudes. When the skilled workers became knowledge workers, the whole factory was different. One frontline old-timer said, "It's like they opened the window and we can breathe." Another described the foremen under the new team-based approach: "They're no longer policemen, but advisers."[36]

In both situations, the workers without buttons were just skilled workers. They had to ask permission. But the people with the buttons were knowledge workers. They were empowered.

The point here is simple: Most of the new breed of volunteers want to be treated like knowledge workers. They want to be able to make empowered decisions. They don't want to always "ask their managers."

This new breed of volunteer wants to do it their way. You can follow all of the steps of recruitment (Chapters 1 to 4) and motivation (Chapter 5), but if you don't master this chapter, you'll still have a high turnover rate. Then other organizations with similar missions—and there are probably a few out there—will end up with your volunteers.

Why Is This Important?

The whole concept of empowerment is important because in the 1980s, a major shift took place in the workplace—the shift from skilled worker to knowledge worker. Because many of your volunteers experienced that shift, you need to make sure you treat your volunteers like knowledge workers, not skilled workers.

What's the difference? Let's take a quick look at both groups:

Skilled workers. Skilled workers don't make decisions. They merely do what they're told to do. When questions come to them that fall outside their job descriptions, they refer to their supervisors. You might call this the "delegation level" of workers.

Knowledge workers. Knowledge workers don't ask their supervisors. The workers are empowered to make decisions. You might call this the "empowerment level" of workers.

By empowering your volunteers, you'll keep them. In fact, we think this is the greatest motivation and volunteer management skill you can learn.

Here's how it works:

Juggling

Let's say that Jim, one of your office volunteers, walks toward you holding a football. Unfortunately, your organization isn't the NFL. It's not even a local rec league. This football represents a "problem." Jim says, "While you were gone on vacation last week, I had a problem with one of our members."

As he explains the problem and asks for your help, you make the mistake that many managers make and respond, "Let me think about it and I'll get back to you." As soon as you speak those words, Jim no longer has to deal with the problem. He hands off the football to you and leaves feeling great because he's just unloaded that problem on you.

Let's say that you'd just come back from vacation and hadn't even reached your desk. You were carrying a "football" of your own before Jim gave you his. Your own football might have been an idea you got on vacation for a dynamic volunteer staff meeting, and you were determined to start planning it immediately. But now you're juggling two different footballs —a project and a problem, and you've only been back to work for seven minutes.

Not three minutes later, you're sitting at your desk when you get an email from Quincy. You're working on a project together and he needs you to call one of your contacts to see if your organization can use their facility. Within 20 minutes you're juggling 10 other footballs that you've taken from your membership, your staff, your volunteer teams, several board members, email, faxes, and voicemail. Have you ever tried to juggle 10 footballs?

How do you juggle these multiple problems, projects, concerns, ideas, and emergencies? You don't! Your volunteers are more than capable—and eagerly waiting—to take some of those footballs and run with them.

The Importance of the Volunteer Manager

This chapter is about managing. Just because volunteers say yes, your job isn't done. As a volunteer manager, you must actually manage or all of your recruiting will be in vain when volunteers quit.

Why do people quit?

Simple: volunteer managers.

Of course, there are two sides to that story.

The manager's side. Volunteers never do the job right! I get so discouraged with the lack of follow-through from volunteers that I just want to do the job myself or hire someone to do it right.

The volunteers' side: We're tired of continually asking for permission to make decisions or handle problems. We're not stupid. Frankly, if we need to make a decision—we're so sick of asking that we're going to just do it anyway. As they say, "It's easier to ask for forgiveness than permission."

Sound familiar?

We see this frequently. Volunteers feel frustrated with the power structure and plunge ahead making decisions without advising leadership. This wouldn't be so bad if they were equipped and empowered to make these decisions. But since they aren't, conflict escalates and either the manager or the volunteer eventually quits.

On the other hand, managers are constantly discouraged with the lack of follow-through from volunteers. We want to give volunteers more responsibility if only they would do a complete job. If you're a volunteer manager, you've been there. So how can you begin depending on your volunteers and have confidence that the job will be done correctly?

Successful Handoffs

The answer is making skillful and successful handoffs. As you juggle multiple projects, deadlines, decisions, daily tasks, and emergencies with volunteers, the handoff process is a vital skill.

The new breed of volunteer wants to be empowered. They don't just want to rubber-stamp your ideas and programs. They want to take responsibility and manage those programs. But the new breed of volunteer also carries a lot of their own "footballs," and sometimes—many times—your priorities are not your volunteers' priorities.

So how can you hand off without fumbling?

Six Rules of Empowerment

When you learn successful handoff skills as a volunteer manager, your volunteers will take the ball and run. And if you follow these six rules of empowerment, you can have confidence that they won't drop the ball.

Rule One: Don't take the football—give it away. In the story above, Jim handed you his football—he gave you his problem. And you made the mistake of taking it. When you said, "Let me think about this problem, and I'll get back to you," you were responsible for the next move. You delegated the football to yourself. You received the football instead of handing it off.

So let's say that you wake up one day, drink a different brew of coffee, and realize, "Why am I taking on everyone else's problems, questions, and decisions?" So you take another sip of that particularly good coffee and decide to make a change.

Now when you walk down the hall and Jim approaches you with a problem, you ask him, "Jim, do you have any ideas for handling this problem?" He might just say, "In fact, I've though about it, and I have several ideas." So you talk about it for a few minutes and decide on a plan of action. As you walk to your office, you say to yourself, "Self, this is great—I gave Jim the football. He has the next move."

You like this feeling, so you keep drinking this new kind of coffee. At your next meeting, Tabitha, another volunteer, approaches you and raises a question. You're about to respond, "Let me think about it and I'll get back to you," but you take a sip of coffee from your thermos and remember what happened with Jim. So you ask, "Tabitha, have you thought about what we should do?"

Tabitha says something that almost makes you drop your coffee. She says, "Actually, I haven't, because usually you want us to just bring these problems to you so you solve them correctly." When she says the word "correctly," her head tilts a bit to the side.

A couple of sips of coffee later, you realize that Tabitha was being somewhat sarcastic with that head tilt. What she was really saying is that you're a bit of an idiot for ignoring all the wisdom of the group and not trusting anyone else to make a decision.

The sad fact is, Tabitha's right. Organizational leaders who rely on volunteers often like to keep all the responsibility for themselves; they believe that the weight of the organization falls on their shoulders.

You immediately realize two things: (1) You need to stop taking handoffs, and (2) you really need to buy more of this amazing coffee!

So you take a deep breath and say, "Tabitha, we are going to change that today. I want you to think of several possible ways to solve that problem, and let's talk later this week. When is a good time for us to talk?" And you set up a meeting.

Don't take handoffs. Instead, hand your volunteers the football.

Rule Two: Label each handoff as either delegation or empowerment. A huge difference exists between empowerment and delegation, but they do have one thing in common: *responsibility*. Who's responsible for the ball?

There are two levels of handing off the ball:

Level One: Talk to me first, and then determine the next move. This is the delegation level.

Level Two: Make the next move, and then tell me about it. This is the empowerment level.

You can sum up the difference between delegation and empowerment in one question: Do I have to ask my manager?

Delegated volunteers *must* ask. They're not empowered to act on their own. Empowered volunteers *don't* have to ask. They make decisions, solve problems, and create solutions without running every question up the chain of command.

In the story above, you made progress when you didn't take the ball from Jim and Tabitha; however, you weren't empowering them. You were setting up the next moves at a delegation level. You really didn't empower either of them because they were still talking to you first about what to do. This is delegation, not empowerment. Empowerment is a whole different level.

To truly empower, you'll need to learn to say to Jim and Tabitha, "Why don't you just handle those problems and then get back to me with what you're doing." When you say those words, you ascend to a whole new level. You're not talking through decisions and actions beforehand; the volunteers report the results to you, after they happen. This is true empowerment.

How can you empower your volunteers to make wise "next moves" with confidence?

Glad you asked. Take a look at our next rule.

Rule Three: Secure the handoff. OK, so it's wonderful to have all of these volunteers running around making creative decisions and handling problems—until things get out of hand! Volunteers can make poor decisions and then you have to spend extra time unraveling tangled messes. Empowerment is scary.

Empowerment sounds wonderful on paper. But in reality, the unknown of empowerment can be stressful. If you've been burned when you've empowered a volunteer, chances are that you then overreacted and set up tight lines of control. We've all done it. But then it happens again—we become overwhelmed with all that we're juggling and our volunteers become frustrated with the roadblocks to all of their ideas.

The solution is to start all of your volunteers at the delegation level and move them to the empowerment level as soon as you can trust them to be empowered. When you discuss a problem or decision with a volunteer, go through your options right there and make a decision.

Back to Jim. He reports to you that the committee for your holiday event has run into a problem with the venue, and it's going to cost a lot more than you've budgeted. You ask Jim to come up with several options and discuss them with you before his next committee meeting. When you talk the next day, he presents the options and you agree on the one that will work best. Jim then presents this idea to the committee.

This is still delegation. As the manager, you're still in control. Jim did the legwork, but you pretty much made the decisions. The fact that you're still making decisions at this point isn't bad, because the discussion you had with Jim is a way to train and mentor him.

However, it's time to empower Jim. The goal is to get him to the point—as soon as you can—where you can say to him, "Jim, you've got a great committee. Why don't you brainstorm with your committee, come up with several ideas, and make a decision. Let me know after your meeting what you decide because we need to get the word out."

This is empowerment.

How long does the transition from delegation to empowerment take? It depends on Jim. Some people are quick studies because of their experience and expertise, and they'll be at an empowerment level very quickly. People new to your organization need some time to understand the culture. But for the most part, volunteers don't want to run to the executive director or volunteer manager about every decision. They want to be able to make decisions. Of course, there are exceptions—some people don't want to make decisions, but the new breed of volunteer wants to be empowered.

We defined the empowerment level as "make the next move, and then tell me about it." Don't forget to stress the "tell me about it." Set a checkup point. You need reports from your empowered volunteers.

Some managers do this with regular meetings, often called the daily check-in, with team leaders (such as Jim, who was leading the committee responsible for the holiday event). The daily check-in is a schedule-oriented, administrative meeting that lasts no more than five or 10 minutes (like a huddle). The purpose is simply to keep team members aligned and to provide a daily forum for activity updates and scheduling. In your organization, a weekly conference call where team leaders give brief updates on their "tell me about it" responsibilities will be enough. You also might say, "Let's get together for lunch next week and you can tell me about what your team decided." Or you could say, "Let's talk tomorrow and you can give me an update about your committee meeting. When should I call you?" That establishes a mutual time for your meeting.

Stephen Drew, former chief curator of the California State Railroad Museum, says that his organization relies heavily on empowered leadership of their volunteers. He told us about a retired project manager from Aerojet who became the project manager for a restoration project at the museum, leading a team of paid staff and six volunteers. We asked Stephen how he makes sure that projects like these don't go in the wrong direction. After all, sometimes when a professional runs with something, they head down a path that you didn't want to travel. Stephen said:

In this case, we meet on a weekly basis to make sure that he doesn't get too far ahead of us. And we're a little different than the aerospace industry—things don't need to be at the same level of precision when we're dealing with big old steam locomotives that are the size of dinosaurs. Good, effective communication is the best way to keep things on track. We don't leave volunteers out there by themselves for more than a week before we dial them up and get some feedback.

It's imperative that you and empowered volunteers regularly discuss what's happening. Continuous feedback is essential as a motivator, and it's an effective method for determining the next move.

For additional help holding empowered volunteers and teams accountable, go to the "Sample Project Charter" on page 226.

Keep in mind that some volunteers will always stay at the delegation level. But many volunteers will want to be empowered and won't continue working with you if you don't empower them. Your job as a manager of the new breed of volunteer is to move as many volunteers as possible toward knowledge workers at the empowerment level.

Rule Four: Break down tasks into manageable goals. Even when they're empowered, your volunteers might fumble the ball if a task is too overwhelming. So what can you do with big tasks that your volunteers will encounter? Do you just do the big ones yourself?

No, simply break down tasks into manageable goals. As a manager, you probably already do this for planning projects, but it's easy to forget about it for empowering and delegation.

TOM I'll never forget when Michael Jordan came back to basketball after playing baseball. Basketball analyst Peter Vecsey asked Jordan if he could pick up where he left off before he "retired," averaging 32 points a game. Jordan's response was classic. He answered, "Why not, that's only 8 points a quarter."[37]

JONATHAN TOM When we feel crushed by the magnitude of the projects we're trying to manage, "32 points" is overwhelming. But if we can break down the projects to "8 points a quarter," they're really not that bad.

The key word is *manageable*. Much of management is insight about what's manageable for the volunteer—and for yourself. Some volunteers can manage huge next moves. Others can't. As a manager, you have to be careful not to micromanage the mover and shaker who wants to take a whole project and run with it. At the same time, you'll need to be careful to not overwhelm others.

TOM I loved working with Bill, who could handle big projects. I never broke down his projects. We were building a new office complex and using a lot of volunteer help. Bill served as the volunteer chairman of the building project. He and I met once a month for an early breakfast. We'd draw plans on paper napkins (that shows you the quality of restaurants we ate at), and Bill would run with the project. We met for a year and he literally updated the project on a napkin. I loved it! For Bill, the manageable task was "build a building within this budget."

"Elliot," however, was nothing like Bill. I was working as a consultant for a trade association of 1,000 members in California, and the executive director kept telling me about his problem with Elliot, who needed guidance on every little decision.

Elliot was the chairman of a committee responsible for finding all the workshop leaders and keynote speakers for the association's conventions. He was also responsible for developing regional continuing education programs.

Elliot drove all the office staff crazy. He wanted to meet with the executive director once a week (unfortunately, Elliot lived in Sacramento and dropped by the association office weekly to see the executive director). The secretaries began to tease each other, "Elliot's here," they'd all moan. Elliot was a high-maintenance, high-involvement, very difficult volunteer who wanted approval on every tiny step. It got to the point where the staff joked that he wanted them to approve the paper color for the meeting minutes.

For more on "Managing or Canning High-Maintenance Volunteers," go to Chapter 8.

Finally, the executive director sat down with Elliot and outlined his projects for the next month, breaking the tasks down into small and manageable steps. He told Elliot to run with the project and they could meet in a month. It worked! The director found that if he met with Elliot once a month and they outlined his next steps, Elliot could handle it.

JONATHAN **TOM** **Rule Five: Don't take the football if you can't do anything about it.** This rule of empowerment helps you determine if the ball is even worthy of the handoff. Too many coaches and volunteers are hauling around footballs that they shouldn't have received in the first place.

Even if you're 2 inches shorter than you'd like to be, you don't have a height problem. Why? Because you can't do anything about it. If you can't do anything about a problem in your organization, then quit carrying around that burden! Instead, learn to focus only on the problems that you can control. To paraphrase Steven Covey from his book *The 7 Habits of Highly Successful People*, when we focus on the problems we cannot control, we empower them to control us.[38]

As a volunteer manager, you might be trying to hand off a football that you shouldn't have accepted to begin with. Don't let it waste time cluttering up your desk—or your life, for that matter. It's a lot like following that simple time-management rule of handling paperwork just once. When you pick up a piece of mail, a contract, or a memo, decide what to do with it immediately. Don't file it away to do later. Then it will just sit there in the "to-do" box for a couple of months—until you trash it. Learn to trash it, file it, or answer it immediately (if possible). And only put in your "to-do" box what you'll get to that week.

The same holds true with projects your volunteers bring to you. Decide if they're even worthy of adding to your projects.

Rule Six: Develop good handoff skills to avoid disaster. Bad habits have disastrous results. When you're only juggling one object, you can get away with bad habits like procrastination, tardiness, disorganization, or lack of planning. But when your work and responsibilities begin to expand, these bad habits will catch up with you.

We worked with an employee who was the manager of a huge volunteer program (with responsibility for more than 200 volunteers). She was a very talented manager who "got by" for years with her talent and relational ability. Later, she became overwhelmed because her talent allowed her to be promoted beyond her ability to manage multiple responsibilities. Her bad habits began to surface: She was always late, she procrastinated, and she avoided conflict by not returning calls to volunteers. Once her responsibilities grew, she was overwhelmed. She finally resigned from her position because her organization was losing volunteers every week.

THE SIX RULES OF EMPOWERMENT

Rule One: Don't take the football—give it away

Rule Two: Label each handoff as either delegation or empowerment

Rule Three: Secure the handoff

Rule Four: Break down tasks to manageable goals

Rule Five: Don't take the football if you can't do anything about it

Rule Six: Develop good handoff skills to avoid disaster

More Volunteers, Less Stress

That's right. If you can master these six rules, you'll experience two things: more volunteers and less stress.

You'll retain more volunteers because empowered volunteers are content volunteers. Most people quit managers, not organizations. The volunteer manager who learns to master the six rules of empowerment will have a much greater retention rate.

The rules of empowerment will also reduce your stress. If you're working nights and long weekends, perhaps you're trying to do too much yourself—afraid someone else will drop the ball. You need to master these rules of empowerment to reduce your stress level, and trust your volunteers to do the great work they want to do for your cause.

USING A NEW BREED OF TECHNOLOGY

Social Media, Wikis, Texting...and the Virtual Volunteer

Today's volunteer doesn't need a day planner, a watch, a computer, or even a landline...*they just need a smartphone.*

What's next? Real-time hologram projections of my board members at our board meetings?

JONATHAN I almost hesitate to write a chapter about technology, in fear that by the time it goes to print, this stuff will already be out of date. You might be amazed by how much we had to totally revamp this chapter for the second edition of the book. So much has changed in just five years.

- The younger generation has grown less fond of email, primarily using texting or social networking instead.

- MySpace® no longer is the social networking powerhouse among young people, and Facebook has truly become king (93 percent of 12- to 17-year-old social media users have Facebook; 24 percent have MySpace).[39]

- In 2012, Pinterest® quickly became a major player on the social network scene, especially with women.

- Smartphone ownership is quickly approaching the 50 percent mark, which has boosted mobile browsing to new levels (53 percent of 18- to 24-year-olds own smartphones, while 64 percent of 25- to 34-year-olds own them).[40]

- The time people spend on apps per day finally surpassed traditional web browsing.[41]

I can only imagine what new developments in technology will emerge in the next five years. (Personally, I'd settle for a soft-serve ice cream dispenser in every vehicle!)

JONATHAN **TOM** So how do advances in technology affect the world of volunteerism? Perhaps that's like asking, "How did the invention of the plane change world travel?"

The new breed of volunteer communicates faster and more efficiently, mobilizing the masses more than ever before. Consider what happened in Egypt in 2011, when digital crowdsourcing played a major role in toppling a whole government. This wasn't the first time in history a government had been toppled by "the people." "It is a truism in political science that successful revolutions are born in the streets—from the Boston Massacre of March 1770 and the storming of the Bastille in Paris in July 1789, to the streets of Cairo in January and February 2011," Sam Gustin of Wired writes. "What has shocked most observers of the current Egyptian scene is the sheer speed with which the regime fell—18 days."[42] The organization of today's revolutions just transformed from analog to digital.

Wael Ghonim, a young Google® executive who became a symbol of Egypt's pro-democracy uprising after he launched the original Facebook page credited with sparking the initial protest, is quoted in Gustin's Wired article as calling the Egyptian upheaval "Revolution 2.0." He credited Facebook and its young founder, Mark Zuckerberg, as an inspiration.

What made the difference is "crowdsourcing"—mobilizing the collective power of volunteers by the use of the social media. Rafat Ali, a social media expert and founder of paidContent, told Wired that a variety of social media contributed to the Egyptian uprising.

"Facebook definitely had a role in organizing this revolution," Ali told Gustin for the Wired article. "It acts like an accelerant to conditions which already exist in the country. Twitter and YouTube serve as amplification for what's happening on the ground. And they directly affect Western media coverage."

Sascha Meinrath, director of the New America Foundation's Open Technology Initiative, made similar statements to Wired: "In the same way that pamphlets didn't cause the American Revolution, social media didn't cause the Egyptian revolution. Social media have become the pamphlets of the 21st century, a way that people who are frustrated with the status quo can organize themselves and coordinate protest, and in the case of Egypt, revolution."

Tweets and Facebook posts may be an effective way to topple a corrupt government, but can they help the director of volunteers in recruiting and leading volunteers? Can we use technology to enlist volunteers, promote an event, or mobilize members for a cause?

If you want impact, then the answer is yes—because let's face it, making a difference is what most executive directors and volunteer leaders are all about.

In this chapter we are going to focus on the use of technology in mobilizing the power of volunteers, specifically:

- Social networks and volunteers

- Wikis

- Text messages and email

- Using technology for training

- Your website

- The virtual volunteer

Social Networks and Volunteers

A 2011 study by the Pew Research Center's Internet & American Life Project *(The Social Side of the Internet)* found that social media users are more likely to be active in volunteer groups: 82 percent of social network users and 85 percent of Twitter users are group participants.[43] This report raises a very important question for those who manage volunteers:

How can you take advantage of the social media opportunity to enhance your volunteer community?

Entire books have been written on this subject, but for now, let's scratch the surface by showing you a few examples of how to use some of the current "major players" in the social networking world:

Facebook

Facebook is truly the king of all social network sites.

Scratch that. Right now, Facebook is king of all websites—period.

Americans actually spend more time on Facebook than they do on any other U.S. website.[44]

Every nonprofit really should have a Facebook page where people can "Like" the organization, look at videos or photos, and keep updated with current information. A Facebook page also provides a fast-response format for feedback or discussion. Many organizations will even post questions that members can respond to and discuss.

Another way to use Facebook is to create buzz for an organization, event, or movement. President Obama's campaign did this well in the 2008 election. But you don't have to be as big as a national political party to make an impact with Facebook. Even the smallest organizations can use it to help spread the word about their causes.

One of the simplest ways to do this is to build a Facebook page about an exciting project or event. Invite people to take a peek at what's going on, and encourage them to invite their friends.

TOM In February 2012 I was on a volunteer team working with schools and churches in Uganda. Many of the team members built networks of donors, raising a few thousand dollars to go on the trip. Communication with these donors was key, both before and during the trip.

One of our team members, a manager from Intel® , created a Facebook page about our trip. Every day on the trip he would post

135

pictures and short videos that were viewed by donors and family members across the globe—sometimes just minutes after being posted. People who saw the posts and pictures immediately responded with encouragement. Those daily contacts between our team, our donors, and our families back home were a huge encouragement.

JONATHAN I was one of those family members viewing those Facebook posts. It's interesting to see the contrast between this trip and the trip Dad took to South Africa over a decade ago. On that last trip we heard from him once the whole trip—a quick phone call to let us know that he hadn't been eaten by an alligator. This trip we were watching video of Dad and his team of volunteers just minutes after an event occurred.

It's amazing how technology like this has opened up the channels of communication in the volunteer community.

JONATHAN TOM But Facebook isn't the only social networking site that helps organizations communicate with their volunteers or donors...

Twitter

When the floodwater destroyed huge parts of Nashville, Tennessee, in May 2010, the Rev. Pete Wilson tweeted a need for volunteers, hammers, trash bags, and brooms, and hundreds of people showed up to start relief work in and around a badly flooded Nashville. "I love being able to mobilize so many volunteers...so quickly," said Wilson, who has more than 54,000 Twitter followers. "I love that power of communication."[45]

Create a Twitter account for your project, and ask volunteers to "follow" you. Share last-minute project updates. During the project, upload and tweet photos for those who couldn't join you that day, to show them what they're missing.

JONATHAN As an author who provides a constant flow of free ministry resources on our websites, I use Twitter to update my readers about new resources, fun contests, or upcoming workshops or events. I might Tweet...

- New article about teenagers texting while driving: http://bit.ly/cJPjnQ

- Win a copy of my new parenting book. Details here: http://bit.ly/GUhD9v

- Hilarious video of a monkey riding a pig: http://bit.ly/abyAul

- Come hear me this weekend as I teach my "Parenting the Texting Generation" workshop in Chicago: http://bit.ly/moEcr0

(OK, and sometimes I just tweet about really silly videos!)

My friend Doug Fields (a speaker and author) started using Twitter to connect with his readers when he'd travel to a given city. He'll tweet the name and address of a specific pizza place and tell his followers to meet him there "this Friday at 11:30 a.m." Doug's list includes roughly 20,000 followers from around the world. Even if Doug's visiting a small town like Collinsville, Illinois, he'll often have 20 people show up. His readers love the personal attention that Doug gives: an opportunity to meet with them in person! Then he excuses himself to the bathroom—and leaves them all with the check! (OK,

I made that last part up. Last time we ate together, Doug paid! Although, it was McDonald's.)

I've started doing the same thing. Of course, only a handful of people show up—usually homeless people.

YouTube

Some people don't think of YouTube as a social networking site, but it actually functions like one. You can create a page, recruit followers, post videos, and send notice of a new video to your followers. It's interactive because people can rate or comment on videos.

YouTube is the "go to" place for video online, so volunteer organizations are smart to create a YouTube page and post training videos, instructional videos, or publicity videos.

Your organization's YouTube page is a great place to post a video about an upcoming project or event. Create a video that makes a compelling case about why the project is important and asks people to get involved. Don't stop at YouTube; share the video through the project's Facebook page and share it via Twitter, linking your YouTube video.

Other social media

As we mentioned at the beginning of this chapter, it's difficult to write much about technology when the only constant about technology is its rapid change. Each one has different draws and features. A site like LinkedIn® draws many men in the business world, while the very artsy Pinterest currently is drawing more women. Many companies and organizations are seeing incredible benefits from marketing to people through these and other sites. President Obama even launched a Pinterest page in 2012 after seeing the potential that this new social networking site offered.[46]

We need to constantly remain on the lookout for tech-savvy volunteers who can keep us current in how we use social networking technology in our organizations, nonprofits, and ministries.

Wikis

The wiki may be one of the greatest inventions since the lightbulb. A wiki is a prime example of Web 2.0. Forget the old methods of event planning that required making conference calls, printing, stapling, mailing, making more calls, writing in the margins, reprinting, faxing—those days are gone.

TOM Recently I spent a day with the Washington State 4-H Club leadership. To facilitate their statewide planning sessions, the leadership introduced the statewide team members to the concept of a wiki—an online tool that lets a group of people share ideas, files, information, and conversation. Because planning sessions for a statewide organization can be expensive when you consider the cost of travel, hotels, or even videoconferencing equipment, the 4-H leaders began using a wiki to plan their events. They found that they liked the way they could share and collaborate on documents without special software or training. Because the wikis are Web pages, it's simple to provide links to references. Planning team members browse and modify the wiki with nothing more specialized than a Web browser. For conference calls, one person posts a rough document or an agenda online; the others correct and contribute to it in real time.

The beauty of a wiki is that you don't need to master any special training or programming. With most wikis, you simply click on the wiki page's "Edit" button to begin changing the page's content. A click of the "Save" button posts the changes back to the website and updates the wiki, making the assembly of content easy and straightforward—everyone on the team can read (and react to) information being generated and then add modifications or corrections. And because the wiki lives online, the team can work on the planning process at any time, from any location offering an Internet connection.

Many groups use websites such as wikispaces.com to create wikis for their committees, teams, or volunteer projects. Others groups purchase software that allows them to have their own wiki just for their organization. I am a volunteer in musical band. Our director uses special software for our communication. We receive instructions about rehearsal times and programs, and he even attaches MP3s and copies of the music so we can practice before the rehearsal. As a volunteer, I love that tool. I'm sure the leader loves it even more.

JONATHAN   TOM   Volunteer organizations often work so slowly. Use of Web 2.0 tools like the wiki speeds things up because you don't have to waste time sending documents back and forth either physically or through email. Web 2.0 gives more people in the organization greater ownership of the volunteer work. It can remove many barriers of administration and bring more people together on collaborating work. These are just a few examples of how technology can actually help an organization streamline costs and get more of the work done with more people.

Text Message and Email

Texting and email are wonderful tools, yet we have a love-hate relationship with these relatively new sources of communication.

Members of Gen Y don't use email much, unless they have to for school or work. In general, they prefer texting. (Some people might even say that they *overuse* text messaging, abandoning interpersonal elements of communication.) At the same time, many Boomers use email but rarely or never text, all the while despising certain elements of both because these methods of communication seem cold and impersonal to them. Yes, how volunteers interpret communication through these methods is somewhat generational.

Texting has a few more "unspoken rules" than email. It's a little more personal, maybe because our phones are almost always right in our pockets. People already dislike email spam, but texting spam is really despised. A 23-year-old doesn't want to receive a text message during the middle of her graduate class telling her, "It's a beautiful day to go plant a tree!"

Instead, use texting for more personal communication, like an individual request or word of encouragement. *"Calvin, thnx so much for your hlp shooting video yesterday. Just watched your footage- amazing! Thnx Spielberg, U rock!"* Or even, *"Chris, I'm going to the teen center at 3:00 to shoot hoops with a bunch of the middle schoolers. Wanna join us? I'm buying pizza afterward."*

Occasionally you can send an urgent group text with a request like, *"Surprise snowstorm is coming tonight & we expect double the number in our lines at the shelter. We're scrambling for blankets & more food. Let me know if you can help this afternoon!"*

Just don't abuse text messages. You don't want to be "the texter that cried wolf." Your volunteers won't listen when you really need their help.

Email has been around much longer and has its own set of rules. Although it's used casually in many circles, it's a step closer to professionalism than texting. It's also more frequently "spammed" than texting is, which is why many emails might get lost in the spam folder. But email is still a necessary and useful communication tool if you understand its limitations.

In spite of headaches email can cause, it remains a superb way to follow up and document meetings. You can also use it to get feedback and to advertise. However, we have several concerns about using email. So here are our don'ts:

Don't deliver bad news by email. Bad news is only worse when someone doesn't have the guts to say it face to face. The bad-news email can be just another way an "Oh, by the way" manager makes requests. The calendars of most of the new breed of volunteers are way too full, so they don't need more "to do" tasks trickling in. For example, the last thing a busy volunteer conference registrar needs to read when she opens her email is, "Kim, would you put together a crew to prepare 400 extra registration packets for our conference this weekend. We have more people registered than we thought." Don't deliver this kind of news via email *or* text.

To review the weaknesses of "Oh, by the way" managers, go to "Classic Oh, By the Ways" on page 30.

While you don't want to deliver bad news via email or text, you certainly could use the technology to broadcast a "Help" email message that reads, "Good news, bad news. The good news is that 400 more people registered for our conference than we expected. The bad news is that we need to quickly prepare 400 extra registration packets. We need as many volunteers as possible to help us next Thursday (Sept. 13) at 7 p.m. We'll provide pizza. Please respond so we know how much pizza to order."

Don't send a message that you wouldn't want to appear in your local newspaper. Emails aren't necessarily private. Emails are open communication, even if you only send a message to one person. Be careful what you type. Emails aren't confidential and sometimes are even used in lawsuits. You never know where the email will go after you press "Send."

Don't assume your email will be read. If no one responds to your broadcast email, pick up the phone and ask volunteers personally. The younger generations especially, as tech savvy as they are, can be inconsistent about reading email. In Sin Number 1 of the seven sins of recruiting, we noted that a message needs to be communicated five times, five different ways, and when people hear it the fifth time, they often say, "I've never heard that before." Email messages provide just one of those "five ways." Email works well to follow up or document a meeting or decision. But using it as the "first" method of communication might not be effective, and you probably won't get the response you need.

Don't use email to rant or vent your frustrations. Email makes it too easy to get out a quick note to everyone. Don't drop bombs in emails. Think of how often you sit down, whip out your thoughts in an email message, skip proofreading, and quickly hit "send." Even if you sit on your message overnight and labor over the wording, it's easy to produce an angry outburst.

Let's be honest: Great writing is rare. Journalists study and practice for years to learn how to communicate well. Presidents and other elected officials use press secretaries and speechwriters to help them communicate. And even with all their training and expertise, many of these professionals occasionally wish that they hadn't worded a speech or an article the way they did.

Most volunteer managers don't have press secretaries or speechwriters or degrees in writing. Yet they thrash out their frustrations in quick emails that ultimately exacerbate the problem. When you express your opinion—especially when you're angry—emails can be misunderstood and volunteers won't hear your intended message. When you lose the power of facial expressions and vocal inflections, you lose important and essential factors in making your point.

Using Technology for Training

Technology has opened new avenues for training today's new breed of volunteer. The Audubon Society uses the Internet to train its volunteers. When talking with Dan Taylor from Audubon, he told us, "We use WebEx™ to train people. We can bring together 20 people from all over the country for a three-hour session on leadership training using a Web-based connection and this software. Timewise, this is much more efficient than training individuals and smaller groups in various parts of the country."

Similarly, many churches host training sessions via satellite from larger conferences. Megachurches such as Willow Creek and Saddleback broadcast these types of training sessions to churches around the country. In 2012, Willow Creek broadcast its annual Leadership Summit live to more than 200 different Premier Host Sites.

The Internet can also be a source of good training materials. The websites of the organizations we lead (volunteerpower.com and TheSource4YM.com) are loaded with free articles for leaders to print, copy, and use for discussion with volunteer coordinators and volunteers. After everyone reads an article, leaders can spark discussion by asking questions:

- What did you like?

- What did you disagree with? Why?

- What hit you as an "Aha!"?

- What would you like to implement?

- What would you like to know more about or learn how to implement?

For an example of using these kinds of materials for training, go to "Case Study: 'Symptoms of Staff Resistance' " on page 199.

Your Website

Your organization's website serves as a window for the world. Many organizations use members-only pages to present information and benefits for the members. And most organizations include an online form that visitors can fill out to get information and to learn how to become a volunteer.

Sue Hood serves as the connection services director of Willow Creek Community Church in South Barrington, Illinois, a church with more than 20,000 people in weekend attendance. Willow Creek uses a special website as a recruiting tool: willowcreek.org/volunteer. People interested in serving as volunteers fill out the online form, noting the ministry they're interested in, any specific interests or skills, the frequency they want to serve, and what location they desire. Sue told us that the volunteer Web page is their primary communication vehicle, connecting with an average of 500 people a week. She adds that one of the most popular pages on the site is the "Top Ten Volunteer Needs" list, which lets potential volunteers know of the greatest needs.

WEBSITES OFFERING VOLUNTEER MANAGEMENT RESOURCES

energizeinc.com—This site features the work of Susan J. Ellis, author, speaker, and one of the most recognized authorities on volunteer management. The site is filled with free resources for the volunteer manager.

churchvolunteercentral.com—This membership site from Group Publishing helps volunteer leaders recruit and equip volunteers for Christian ministry.

serviceleader.org/virtual—This website is totally dedicated to virtual volunteers and includes resources for volunteer managers who want to create or enhance their virtual volunteer program.

volunteerpower.com—This is Tom's website, and it offers free resources and articles for volunteer managers.

TheSource4YM.com—This is Jonathan's website, which offers youth workers truly free resources to help them reach teenagers, including a "Free Training Tools" page, as well as a huge database of games, team-builders, event and activity ideas, curriculum, articles, and how-to's.

We've just scratched the surface regarding technology. The potential might reach as far as cyberspace itself. Because we must still recruit, screen, motivate, and lead volunteers, technology doesn't really change the duties of volunteer managers. However, cyberspace does open the door to significant changes in how we can do our jobs.

The Virtual Volunteer

Tiffani Hill, volunteers manager with Best Friends Animal Society, manages 600 animal rescue volunteers who respond to disasters around the world. It's a big job, made even bigger by the fact that she's never met any of those 600 volunteers face to face—they're all virtual volunteers. So Tiffani uses five virtual volunteer coordinators to manage the other 600 volunteers. The coordinators do all of their recruiting, screening, scheduling, and even firing online.

If you've never used virtual volunteers, this might sound like a very different world of volunteer management. Even though thousands of organizations involve virtual volunteers,[47] it's still fairly new. Many people don't even know what virtual volunteers are, while others remain skeptical about venturing into an off-site volunteer program that lacks the interpersonal, face-to-face contact.

Six Common Questions About Coaching the Virtual Volunteer

1. Do you have to be a "techie" to start a virtual volunteer program?

Before we define *virtual volunteering*, let's address *technophobia*. Many of us are scared of anything technological. Some of us need to call up our Gen Y son or daughter just to help us figure out the thermostat in our new house.

TOM I admit that when I hear people talking about new technologies, I have mixed feelings. I get excited when I think about some of these fun, new technological gadgets. But I also get a little apprehensive because when I read the owner's manual for my home theater system, I don't have a clue what it means. When I can't get everything adjusted correctly, my wife groans, "I long for the old days when you just turned on the TV and it worked!"

JONATHAN TOM When you think about using anything with advanced technology, do you feel a little bit hesitant? When we talked with Tiffani Hill from Best Friends, we asked if she has a background in technology. She burst out laughing! Tiffani is like most of us: She's a volunteer manager, not an IT specialist. Tiffani is a certified volunteer administrator with no formal technical background. Yet Best Friends hired her to create and manage an online volunteer program.

Tiffani says, "My coordinators have a lot more experience than I do. In fact, they asked about my experience when I was hired, because I don't have a background in technology." Tiffani does have 10 years of experience in the volunteer field, and she came with some really strong credentials for staff programs. Best Friends allowed her to learn the technology "as she went." Other staff members at Best Friends have software backgrounds, and they back up Tiffani and other volunteers. Tiffani admits, "Yes, I've had to learn to swallow my pride and get help with technology at times—even from my volunteers."

JONATHAN Over a decade ago, I was looking for free youth ministry resources and ideas on the Internet but finding very little. Everywhere I clicked, another website offered a handful of freebies but an entire catalog of resources for sale. So I started TheSource4YM.com, a website that provides "truly free" youth ministry resources and ideas.

It exploded, and immediately visitors from around the world who couldn't get enough of these free resources started visiting the site.

I didn't have any money, so I depended on volunteers to help build the website. My brother, my friend Amie, and a teenager named Jason all caught the passion for what I was doing and donated time here and there to add new resources to the site. Usually, I'd email them what I needed done, and they'd add the materials to the site.

Volunteer opportunities began to grow. People from around the world began collecting stuff and submitting it to the website. Youth workers from across the country began building game lists. One volunteer, halfway across the country in Texas, helped develop entire new pages for the site. He turned into a virtual employee for several years. I still haven't met most of these people face to face. All the work was done through the virtual world of the Internet.

Today, I have both virtual volunteers and virtual employees. We do 98 percent of communication through email, and the other 2 percent over the phone.

I find it hilarious that to this day, I know very little about computers and I'd have no clue how to build a website. I call my friends Tom or Troy just to set up a router in my office. I'm technologically impaired, but that's never stopped me from using virtual volunteers.

JONATHAN TOM The fact that many virtual volunteer managers lack a technological background should provide some comfort. Volunteer coordinators can develop a virtual volunteer program and work effectively with the new breed of volunteers without any expertise in technology.

Before we go any further, let's define what a "virtual volunteer" is.

2. What is a virtual volunteer?

Volunteer gurus Jayne Cravens and Susan Ellis answer as follows: "Virtual volunteering refers to volunteer tasks completed, in whole or in part, via the Internet and a home or work computer. It's also known as online volunteering, cyber service, telementoring, teletutoring, and various other names."[48] We've seen online volunteers do tasks like web design, proofreading, writing, creating videos, moderating chat rooms—the possibilities are endless. Online volunteers sometimes work for local organizations; others work thousands of miles away.

However, virtual volunteering isn't limited to online volunteering. It can also include people who work from a distance over the phone or who even use mail. A virtual volunteer might be someone who makes phone calls for an organization from home, or someone who stuffs envelopes and sends out newsletters from home.

A virtual volunteer is simply anyone who donates time to an organization off-site.

3. Why consider virtual volunteers?

Two words: exponential expansion. Cyberspace opens the opportunity to help you accomplish your mission beyond your wildest imagination. The only limitations are the confines of cyberspace—which seem to be beyond comprehension. The virtual volunteer program also expands your volunteer base, and who doesn't want and need more volunteers?

You might think that only national or international organizations use virtual volunteers. But that's not true. The Internet also opens up opportunities to people in your local area who can't volunteer face to face or who prefer tasks they can do at home on their own schedule. Even small organizations can effectively use virtual volunteers.

David Harper is the volunteer coordinator for Epilepsy Ontario, an organization improving the quality of life for people in Ontario, Canada, affected by epilepsy and seizure disorders. David has 3 paid staff, about 10 core volunteers, and another 60 volunteers that help with special events. They recently expanded their volunteer program to include three virtual volunteers, who research and answer questions submitted to the organization's website.

David says, "We receive approximately 12 to 15 inquiries a week. I read over the questions and forward them by email to the virtual volunteer I think can best answer them. One of these volunteers has epilepsy. Another is a recent graduate in psychology. She also speaks French, which is an asset because we get two or three inquiries each week in French."

Why did David recruit these virtual volunteers? Because he now has three quality volunteers who wouldn't be helping his organization if they had to come into the office several days a week.

The Society for the Blind in Sacramento, California, expanded its volunteer program by developing a whole different kind of virtual volunteer: telephone readers. The volunteers read from their homes over the phone into a computerized phone system. Most of the 90 volunteers spend two to three hours a week recording a very specific topic. They find their niche and read from selections they like. Some might read a weekly national newsmagazine. Others read books, grocery ads from the local newspaper, or store ads. The beauty of the virtual reading program is that blind people can dial up to listen anytime they want.

Expanding your volunteer program to include virtual volunteers will open doors to people and possibilities beyond the reach of traditional volunteers.

4. How do you recruit virtual volunteers?

Recruiting, managing, and even firing virtual volunteers is a lot like working with on-site volunteers, except that you do it all from a distance, usually online. You follow all of the principles and methods of recruiting and managing and firing explained in this book—but from a distance.

To review volunteer recruiting methods, go to "Chapter 2: Recruiting the New Breed of Volunteers." To review volunteer management methods and principles, go to "Chapter 6: Empowering Volunteers to Do It Their Way." And to read more about terminating volunteers, go to "Firing High-Maintenance Volunteers."

David, the volunteer coordinator with Epilepsy Ontario, found his three virtual volunteers by advertising free on charityvillage.com, a nationwide site in Canada for posting volunteer opportunities. David personally interviewed the individuals and checked their references.

Regina Brink, volunteer coordinator for the Society of the Blind in Sacramento, recruits virtual volunteers using volunteermatch.com and the United Way. Representatives from her organization also go to volunteer fairs and recruit from local businesses, because some volunteers record their readings during their lunch hours. The prospective readers audition to make sure that they can read well and that that their voices will be easy to listen to. They then spend an hour or two in training, which takes place at the Society for the Blind office.

Leaders from most organizations that use virtual volunteering agree that it's always valuable to have an organization's name out there. Several use websites like volunteermatch.com and energizeinc.com, but most attribute new prospects to word-of-mouth promotion through their active volunteers and staff.

Screening virtual volunteers can be a little more difficult than traditional volunteers. Often, traditional volunteers are already knowledgeable about your organization because they have some natural connection to it. However, with virtual volunteers, this might not be the case. Thanks to the Internet, organizations sometimes reach beyond their philosophical and theological walls to prospective volunteers. This makes the interview process even more important.

Many organizations that use virtual volunteers include an online application for potential volunteers to complete when they see an ad or respond to an online list of volunteer opportunities. You'll want your virtual volunteer application to probe three core areas:

1. Commitment to the philosophy and mission of your organization

2. Computer experience and equipment available

3. Self-motivation

See page 247 for a "Sample Questionnaire for Virtual Volunteers."

5. How do you manage virtual volunteers?

Even when volunteers are self-motivated and disciplined, they still need feedback. "Without feedback you don't know where you stand" is just as essential of a principle for virtual volunteers as for face-to-face volunteers. Virtual volunteer managers should immediately respond to any work that virtual volunteers do. You might simply send a quick email that says, *"Thanks for your report—looks great at first glance. I'll be going over it in a few days and will get back to you. Thanks for all you're doing."*

Sometimes a phone call just to check in is important. Once in a while, send a snail-mail note to say thanks. Volunteers who do everything online understand the effort to send a thank you note by mail. This is especially important with older generations.

To review other ideas for expressing your appreciation to volunteers, go to "Provide Tangible Incentives."

JONATHAN I learned this principle the hard way. I found a phenomenal virtual volunteer and was ecstatic with the work he did. But I forgot to tell him.

Sounds stupid, huh? I didn't even realize it was a problem until six months later when we finally met face to face at a convention. We went to lunch and talked about the organization and the work he was doing. I began telling him how appreciative I was and how much he'd done for our organization. He was shocked. He thought I'd brought him to lunch to "let him go."

I'd made the mistake of communicating with him via email the same way I communicated to traditional volunteers through email. Email is quick and to the point. With traditional volunteers this works fine, because I have opportunities to offer recognition and praise in person. But email is void of even the simplest nonverbal cues, such as excitement when something goes well or a smile of appreciation. This virtual volunteer never received the "face time" that my traditional volunteers did. Further, he was out of the loop in many of our discussions and decisions, so he never felt part of the team.

After this eye-opening lunch, I fixed the situation. I began spending more time—literally just minutes more—when writing emails to him. I took time to draft updates when we made in-house decisions and asked his opinion before meetings so I could share his "two cents." We set up a way for him to join in on key meetings through teleconferencing.

As a result, he began to perform better because of my investment communicating to him. I simply increased the time spent emailing him by just two or three minutes a day, plus a monthly phone call to check in.

6. How do you fire virtual volunteers?

Risk management, important in all volunteer management, becomes especially important when you have to fire a virtual volunteer. You still need to follow the steps you'd take in firing an on-site volunteer, but you'd take the steps online or over the phone.

We talked to one volunteer manager who has had to fire three virtual volunteers. In one of the situations, she kept trying to coach a volunteer who overcommitted, and the volunteer finally crashed. When the volunteer sent an inappropriate letter under the banner of the organization to a high-ranking official, it caused some backlash. The volunteer manager didn't fire the volunteer at first. She called him, worked with him, and gave him a stern warning. However, within a few days following the conversation, he showed no signs of improvement, so she had to let him go. The volunteer manager told us that she had documented everything—all correspondence, all conversations, and letters regarding discipline. She said that if she had to do it over again, she'd do everything the same except that she'd bring another staff person into the room for the phone conversations, which were otherwise undocumented.

To read more about specific steps of performance coaching and— if necessary—firing, go to "Chapter 8: Managing or Canning High- Maintenance Volunteers." Most of the principles listed there can also be done online or over the phone.

REMINDERS FOR VOLUNTEER MANAGERS USING TECHNOLOGY

- You don't have to be a "techie" to use virtual volunteers

- Embracing virtual volunteers can exponentially increase your volunteer base

- Managing virtual volunteers is just like face-to-face management, except you carry it out remotely

- Technology—including email, training, and websites—can enhance any volunteer program

Looking Back

Using technology and engaging virtual volunteers are ultimate examples of the new breed of volunteers that this book is all about. Whether on-site or online, these volunteers are extremely busy, desire to do volunteer work according to their schedules, and want to be empowered to do it their way. If volunteer managers are willing to take the risk, cyberspace opens countless doors for creativity, innovation, and expansion.

CHAPTER 8

MANAGING OR CANNING HIGH-MAINTENANCE VOLUNTEERS

Performance Coaching the Volunteer From Hell

Have you ever asked the following about your volunteers: "Am I better off with them or am I better off without them?"

Sometimes, it feels like volunteers have nothing better to do than to make our lives miserable. You know the kind—the annoying woman who makes everyone in the office feel awkward, the loose cannon who's likely to get your organization sued, the gossip who can't keep his mouth shut, or the micromanaging board member who questions your every move.

Do you keep 'em or can 'em?

Let's look at each option.

Managing High-Maintenance Volunteers

In every workshop on volunteer management we lead, someone asks, "How do you fire a volunteer?"

Let's not get too hasty. First, perhaps we should ask the question, "*Should* we fire a volunteer?"

Volunteers don't get paid, so why not just let flakey volunteers continue doing whatever they want to do *when* they want to? After all, a little work is better than no work. Sounds fine. But what if a volunteer graduates a little bit beyond flakey?

Do any of these high-maintenance volunteers look familiar?

Know-it-all Nick: Nick is a very poor listener. Nick is a retired Air Force colonel. He has a wealth of experience but expects others to follow his orders. His motivation for volunteering is his basic need to lead and to solve problems. In his retirement, he loves to sit on boards and give advice. Nick sits in your organization's board meetings and quickly tells you what to do about a problem. Of course, he's experienced every problem and will tell you about five stories of how he solved each one. He'll quickly outline solutions and tell you what to do.

The problem with Nick is that he really is knowledgeable. But life in your organization is nothing like life in the Air Force or in private-sector business. Working with volunteers isn't about giving orders. Yet Nick has some fantastic contacts—and he's a big donor.

Helpful Hanna: Hanna is a hard worker. She's motivated by her strong desire to help others. She can't do enough for you and the organization. She's a caring person who loves to be involved in the personal lives of people. She consistently cooks meals and delivers them to members of your organization when they're going through a tough time. Hanna can be described as the classic "people person."

However, Hanna can't keep her convictions to herself. She imposes them on others. She calls you at home at least twice a week with a concern about one of your organization's members. She lets you know every time one of your volunteer receptionists has an aunt whose next-door neighbor's cousin's boss was just diagnosed with the shingles—and thinks you'll probably want to visit that person. She works hard and believes that you want to be aware of all of the problems in everyone's lives. But Mother Teresa probably would have run from Hanna...or shot her!

Negative Nancy: Nancy constantly complains about the people on the board, the people on her committee, the way the organization spends its money, and the brand of sweetener in the break room. Nancy relentlessly tells you that she doesn't know how you deal with all of these problems. But behind your back, she tells everyone else that she doesn't understand how they deal with you!

In brainstorming sessions Nancy makes statements like, "We tried that five years ago, and it didn't work" and "That will never work in a nonprofit organization" and "We'll never get our members to buy in to that program."

Dangerous Dan: Dan might make a great Hollywood stunt man, but he's a lousy addition to your children's ministry. At first, you thought that his antics were funny. Kids love him because he always picks them up and tosses them in the air. But then the tosses got a little higher—in rooms with ceiling fans!

Dan is high-risk. He lives life on the edge. Unfortunately, he brings the children in your ministry to the edge with him. Not a month goes by without a parent complaint. No matter how many times you talk with him, Dan doesn't seem to respond.

If you have high-maintenance volunteers like Nick, Hanna, Nancy, and Dan, you've probably wondered if your organization would be better off without them. But what if you could improve their performance? Wouldn't that be better than just canning them? Let's face it, volunteers aren't always easy to find. So perhaps you can discover ways to manage these high-maintenance volunteers without having to go home frustrated and taking it out on the dog.

We recommend performance coaching. The goal of volunteer performance coaching is to bring the volunteer's performance up to the standards of expectation. Try the following coaching steps to turn around a high-maintenance volunteer. At each step, you need to decide if this volunteer is worth the high maintenance.

Step 1
Step in Their Shoes

Before you do anything else, step in your volunteer's shoes for a moment. Perhaps she's a high-level executive used to having someone quiver at the mere sound of her voice. Or perhaps the volunteer is a midlevel manager who is frustrated or trapped in his work and is looking for validation and purpose in your organization. As a result, he's overly eager and overly helpful to the point where you feel suffocated. If you look at the situation from the viewpoint of these volunteers, you can start to understand the motivation behind their actions—you'll start to empathize with them.

TOM In one of the management workshops I lead, I have participants do a listening technique exercise. I ask each person to play the role of a very specific high-maintenance volunteer. In the role-play, the manager assumes this role for about 15 minutes—acting, talking, and reacting like a problem volunteer.

The results are often revealing. Some managers report that they've never taken the time to feel what a difficult volunteer is feeling. Others say that they start to see what this volunteer is saying. Of course, this isn't always the case. Sometimes the exercise just reinforces that this high-maintenance volunteer is really troubled and out to make life miserable for the manager.

 The next time you're dealing with a high-maintenance volunteer, give this step a shot. Sometimes this exercise is all it takes to understand what the volunteer is going through.

After you've taken a few minutes to put yourself in your volunteer's shoes, move to the next step.

Step 2

Ask, "Are There Valid Complaints Behind Their Actions?"

Look for the kernel of truth in the actions of your difficult volunteer. Instead of making a mental list of "101 ways to get rid of this volunteer," take a moment and ask yourself, "What is this person's complaint?"

Most volunteers either don't feel listened to or don't feel appreciated. The only way you'll really know is by listening. Listen carefully to what they're saying—both verbally and nonverbally. Try not to interrupt or defend yourself or your organization. Hear them out. Have an in-depth phone call, go out to lunch or coffee, or have them ride with you to a meeting. Get them talking. Listen for the clues. What are their pet peeves?

Use the *facts, feeling, and future* probing method of listening. This method tells you what they observe, how they feel about it, and what they think they can do about it. Wouldn't you love to know those three things from your volunteers?

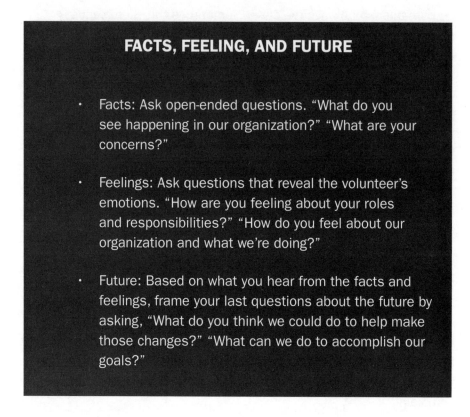

FACTS, FEELING, AND FUTURE

- Facts: Ask open-ended questions. "What do you see happening in our organization?" "What are your concerns?"

- Feelings: Ask questions that reveal the volunteer's emotions. "How are you feeling about your roles and responsibilities?" "How do you feel about our organization and what we're doing?"

- Future: Based on what you hear from the facts and feelings, frame your last questions about the future by asking, "What do you think we could do to help make those changes?" "What can we do to accomplish our goals?"

Get troubled volunteers talking about other organizations they're involved with. Ask what those other groups seem to be doing right. Find out if the volunteer has suggestions for implementing those ideas into your organization.

Step 3

Determine How You Should Respond

Once you've listened carefully, you'll need to respond. Perhaps you need to apologize for something you could have done better. Even if you feel that you've apologized plenty of times before, it obviously didn't get through enough to diffuse the volunteer's concerns.

Or you might choose to use performance coaching (one-on-one meetings that happen between managers and volunteers) to resolve concerns. Some organizations do this through informal performance reviews. For example, Steven Drew, former chief curator of the California State Railroad Museum, said that experienced docents giving tours of the museum sometimes begin embellishing the history. A lead docent regularly joins tour groups to critique and give docents feedback. Steve said that they don't want the guides to be tied to a specific script, but they don't want them inventing history either.

Performance coaching provides a proactive way to interact with and respond to your volunteers. Many organizations don't have meetings like these, opting to put out fires as they appear with volunteers. That's OK, if you don't mind getting burned once in a while.

When problems with your volunteers emerge, try the following suggestions to save the situation for yourself, the volunteer, and the organization.

Frame the problem. If you have several problems with a high-maintenance volunteer, you might be tempted to tell him how much time and energy he's costing you. Don't give in to that temptation. Instead, ask yourself this question, "Do I have a problem volunteer or a volunteer with a problem?" The problem volunteer will probably never change. Problem volunteers have a new crisis every week. We've heard these people referred to as VDPs—very draining people. As the name implies, all they seem to do is drain your energy.

But a volunteer with a problem might be going through something in his personal life. If you learn that you have a volunteer with a problem, then you'll want to be there for and help him through it.

That's part of the community of volunteers, and you need to share the load.

If you have a problem volunteer with a new crisis each week, you'll need to move to the next suggestion.

Enforce the rules. Keep standards high. You might have volunteers who don't understand that the organization's rules need to be followed. Youth volunteers and interns in particular test rules as part of their self-expression. In our experience, when a manager enforces rules (like being on time), 80 percent of volunteers say, "It's about time," 10 percent don't understand, and 10 percent say, "I'll test this to see if our manager really means it."

When you allow high-maintenance volunteers to slide by, active volunteers become discouraged because they have to pick up the load. Remember, the new breed of volunteer won't tolerate incompetence or indifference from other volunteers. They don't want to waste their time working with people who aren't professional or committed to the mission of the organization. They'll appreciate you holding the standard high. Chris Radloff, from Camp Timber-lee, says this: "I'd rather have fewer good volunteers than a lot of mediocre volunteers. You're better off with just two great volunteers than two great volunteers and four mediocre ones. The mediocre volunteers will chase the good ones away."

If you've developed a specific project charter and laid out clear expectations, you can talk to the volunteer when those expectations aren't being met.

For a "Sample Position Charter," go to page 219, and for "Sample Volunteer Expectations," go to page 223.

For example, Jacob is the chairman of a fundraising event. But he doesn't come to board meetings prepared with a report. Instead, he shares a few ideas he jots down while everyone gets settled. As a result, the meetings are chaotic and often unproductive. Jacob's volunteer manager needs to meet with Jacob and give him some specific checkpoints to hold him accountable and to help him do his job better. His position charter becomes the criteria for the performance-coaching meeting. At some point, the manager needs to ask Jacob if he'll be able to fulfill his assignment, or if the organization should find someone else.

Offer a timeout. This isn't for punishment, but for refreshment. Problem volunteers might have lost their passion for the organization or their roles and may need a rest. They might not realize that they're burned out and that a sabbatical could be in order. If possible, swap volunteers with another organization for a month or two. Your volunteer might come back inspired with a new vision.

These alternatives are both easier to implement and smarter than deciding to terminate a volunteer. They take into account the many reasons a volunteer behaves inappropriately, and allow for actions without necessarily separating the volunteer from the program.

We strongly urge you to consider the preceding alternatives before firing any volunteer. The goal of performance coaching is to get the project back on target. However, if you take these steps and your volunteer can't get back on target, it's time to find a replacement.

Firing High-Maintenance Volunteers

What if you try all of the above steps, yet decide that your organization is better off without a high-maintenance volunteer? Should you fire her? If so, how do you fire a volunteer when volunteers don't get paid?

Legal issues. Before you have the firing meeting, be sure to check out the legal ramifications of such a decision. Even if you think it can't happen to you, realize that volunteer managers and organizations are always targets for lawsuits. If you're like us, you hate the thought of lawsuits. More than just frustrating, lawsuits can shut down organizations. Laws that govern organizations were written to prevent those with power from taking advantage of that power. To be fair and make sure that volunteers in your organization are treated with respect, you must follow consistent guidelines.

This section is to assist you as you gather legal advice for your particular situation. We're not trying to give legal advice at all. Before you make any legal decisions, it's essential to contact your organization's lawyer. If you lead a small organization, you might be giggling right now, as you think, "We don't have a lawyer. We don't even have a janitor!" However, even small organizations should try to consult legal counsel at least when setting up policies, screening guidelines, and job descriptions. Once these policies and guidelines are in place, you shouldn't have to consult a lawyer every time you blink.

One of the most important ways to prevent the need to "fire" a problem volunteer is to carefully screen volunteers before they get involved. Position charters (job descriptions) and a volunteer manual that every volunteer reads and signs will help your organization be in a legal position of "fairness."

For a "Sample Position Charter," go to page 219.

However, if you find yourself in a position where you do need to fire a volunteer, we recommend following these steps as well:

Document all discussions. When you must hold a "firing" meeting, the more documentation you have—including conditions and policies for termination—the safer you'll be when it comes to legal repercussions. When a volunteer continues to fail to meet your organization's standards, keep a personnel file and write up a brief summary page on each corrective intervention meeting. A summary page might look something like the sample below.

PERFORMANCE COACHING MEETING

Manager: Jon Jackson

Volunteer: Lucky Smith

Discussion: I talked with Lucky about not showing up for his volunteer shift at the information desk on June 5, July 6, and August 14. He said that he had a family emergency in June, was on vacation in July, and just forgot in August. He was sorry and would try to do better. We talked about him getting a replacement when he could not make it. He said he would.

Based on this documentation, everything sounds great—until Lucky does the same thing again the week after the meeting. So what do you do now? Because you've followed all of the steps of "Managing the High-Maintenance Volunteer" and you've documented the failed performance, it's time for the firing meeting. So you call him the next day to set up a meeting and terminate his position.

Hold the firing meeting. When you've finally made the decision to terminate a volunteer, you actually need to communicate that decision to the volunteer. This responsibility of volunteer managers isn't one of the most rewarding parts of the job, and it's usually not a pleasant experience. But here are some tips that might help:

- *Conduct the meeting in a private setting.* Sometimes, volunteer managers try to ease the pain by conducting a firing meeting in a social setting, such as going out to lunch. However, to preserve the professional nature and structure of this meeting, it should never be held in a restaurant or in a car. Sometimes these meetings get emotional, or the volunteer argues and says, "Hey, I'm doing the best I can, and I'm donating my time. Are you really firing me? I can't believe it." A car or restaurant isn't the place for such a disagreement.

- *Be specific.* Some managers use the "sandwich method," placing the message that the volunteer wasn't meeting expectations between praise about what the volunteer did well. The message becomes so vague that the volunteer leaves the meeting wondering if he was fired or offered a job.

One volunteer manager told Steve that his work with kids was fantastic and the inner-city young people loved him, so the organization wanted to put him on the full-time staff. But then the manager said that other staff members were concerned because Steve tended to be late, often didn't show up at all, and they just couldn't depend on him. Words like tended and often were so vague, especially when couched between phrases such as *fantastic* and *put him on full-time staff*, that Steve left the meeting with mixed messages.

Instead, what the manager needed to say was, "Steve, we just can't depend on you. On September 10, 17, and 24, you didn't show up, and we were counting on you. I talked to you about this, and you said you agreed that if you couldn't make the commitment to be there each week, we'd need to replace you. Then you didn't show up the next few weeks, so we've found someone to replace you and we're taking you off our volunteer team. If your schedule and commitments should ever change, please contact us, and we can explore the possibilities of you volunteering with us again."

- *Follow up.* Send a follow-up letter such as the one on the next page to the volunteer stating your appreciation and anything positive that you can say; however, clearly state the decision to terminate the volunteer. Inform staff and other volunteers on the team of the decision. Be sure to keep the details confidential.

VOLUNTEER TERMINATION FOLLOW-UP LETTER

Mr. Lucky Smith
123 Broadway
Centerville, CA 93939

Dear Lucky,

Thank you for your interest and involvement in ABC Organization and the time you spent volunteering as a greeter at our information booth. This is such an important position as we make many public contacts. Your outgoing personality and winsome way with people were real assets to us.

We're so disappointed that your schedule didn't allow you to keep the requirements of the position charter, as outlined in our volunteer personnel manual. As mentioned in our meeting on September 26, we need to seek a replacement for your position and terminate our letter of agreement.

I trust that when your schedule changes, and you feel that you can meet the requirements of this position, we can once again have you be a part of our volunteer team.

Sincerely,

Jon Jackson
Volunteer Manager

Preparing for firing backlash. Sometimes firing is more trouble than the problem of dealing with high-maintenance volunteers. This especially holds true in churches, where people expect leaders to be forgiving and firing sounds vindictive.

JONATHAN I received a letter recently from one of our subscribers on TheSource4YM.com who faced this kind of situation.

Dear Jonathan,

I have a situation I don't know how to handle. We have a 20-year-old sponsor for our middle school group recruited by our previous youth leader. This young woman hasn't been receptive to guidelines about being alone with kids. She won't support another sponsor if a discipline issue arises. She refuses to discuss anything with the adult sponsors. Now, because of a conflict over one of our youth, she's opted to take a break from the group. This was her decision, but she's now meeting with some of the kids and communicating with them by email. Apparently, she's angry with me and the other sponsors and letting the kids in on it. So I now have upset kids, parents, and pastor. I've tried to talk with her but she doesn't want to. I'm fairly new at all of this and want to do the right thing for everyone. To me, her actions say that she's thinking of herself and not the kids. What do you think I should do?

"Debbie"

Here's how I replied:

"Debbie,"

First, let me tell you, I've had one of these too. I call them the Fatal Attraction *staff member—the one you wish you had never started a relationship with. I needed staff desperately and I recruited a similar young woman, bypassing some of the formalities. When I noticed some problems, I talked with her but got no response. So I talked with her again, this time a little more firmly. "I really need you to stop taking these kids out to the dance place to pick up guys!" She didn't get it.*

To make a very long story short, we removed her from our staff. Unfortunately, that isn't the end of the story. She wouldn't go away. She kept going over to kids' houses, visiting them, and taking them out. She started spreading lies about me and some of the other volunteers, trying to get kids to turn against us. What a nightmare! Then she broke into my house and boiled my rabbit! Oh...wait—she didn't do that! That was the movie Fatal Attraction!

I feel your pain, but this is one of those things that you probably can't "fix." You can only "do the right thing" and let time pass. If you do what's right, then no one can say anything against you. Eventually, the situation will pass, and your character will shine through. Keep showing love to the students involved. You won't need to say a word about the issue—your actions will speak more truth.

Fortunately, in my situation, the kids involved with the psycho-staff-person eventually saw the inconsistencies in her life. They even came back and apologized for ever thinking bad about me and other leaders.

Keep up the good work! Let me know how it goes. And don't leave your rabbit outside!

Jonathan

 Firing a volunteer is tough. So again, we want to emphasize that firing should be your last resort, and only consider it when the continued involvement of the volunteer will have a negative impact on your organization.

TOM Have I ever had to fire a volunteer? Yes, but not a highly involved volunteer. When a highly involved volunteer was also a trouble volunteer, I did everything I could to salvage the dignity and resources of that person. Sometimes I went home and complained a lot to my wife about this person, but we always made it work.

I indeed have fired high-maintenance volunteers who didn't fulfill their commitments. And I really didn't lose any sleep over it. Don't waste your time with volunteers who don't do what they commit to doing. Move on.

IN A NUTSHELL

Coaching and firing high-maintenance volunteers involves taking the following steps.

MANAGING

Step 1: Step in their shoes

Step 2: Ask, "Are there valid complaints?"

- Use the "facts, feelings, and future" listening technique

Step 3: Determine how you'll respond

Performance Coaching: Give feedback

- Frame the problem: Do you have a problem volunteer or volunteer with a problem?

- Enforce the rules: Keep the standards high

- Time out: Not for punishment, but refreshment

FIRING

Consider legal implications

Document all discussions

Facilitate the firing meeting

- Hold it in a private place

- Be specific

- Write a follow-up letter

SECTION THREE

THE VOLUNTEER
LEADER

In this role, you understand how to establish the power and passion of
your volunteer team.

Chapter 9: Leading the Successful Volunteer Organization
Mobilize the Collective Power of Volunteers

Chapter 10: Epilogue—A Leadership Case Study
A Fable of How to Do It Right

LEADING THE SUCCESSFUL VOLUNTEER ORGANIZATION

Mobilize the Collective Power of Volunteers

They walked into the room wearing athletic shoes and with whistles hanging around their necks. When we first met this group, they were volunteers who had no money, no power, and no influence. But together they changed a California law—not an easy task, changing legislation. Their story is the story of volunteer passion working at its best.

Who were these people?

Most of them were high school coaches who used to teach driver's education. California had eliminated behind-the-wheel driver's education, and this group got together to see what they could do about it. Their desire? To reverse the rising trend of teenage-driver accidents on California highways. Every day in California, a teenage driver was involved in an accident, many of them with fatalities. But no one was willing to tackle this crisis. Changing legislation was like trying to steer the Titanic with an ice pop stick. But this handful of teachers and coaches, members of the all-volunteer organization, the California Association for Safety Education (CASE), decided to give it a try.

They pulled it off! United in passion, this volunteer group got laws changed that affect every driver whose tires touch a California highway. (Keep reading to find out what they did!)

If you're a volunteer leader, your job is to focus all the passion, energy, and enthusiasm of your volunteers into a successful organization to make a lasting impact.

Leading is different than managing. Leaders set the vision for where an organization is going. Managing paves the road to get it there. Certainly, managers recruit and unleash the passion of individual volunteers. But it takes a leader to mobilize the powerful energy and passion of individual volunteers into a dynamic movement.

We see at least five skills and principles—five essentials of leadership—that volunteer leaders must have to help their organizations be successful. Let's look at how volunteer leaders can excel in each of these areas.

Passion: Where Power Begins

Like the CASE volunteers who changed motor vehicle law in California, most volunteer organizations have something every business would love to have. It's something that government agencies would somehow like to implant in every employee. Volunteer organizations have an advantage that no one else has.

It's called passion. Nothing is more effective than the passionate power of volunteers. When volunteers focus on their cause, they're unstoppable.

TOM Audubon Society members are passionate about birds. They're so passionate, they're called "birders." I was leading a workshop for the National Audubon Society and made the mistake of teaching it outdoors. No one told me that all the members would have binoculars hanging around their necks. Every time a bird flew over or landed in a tree, a hundred pairs of binoculars all pointed to the air and people started talking about the birds. They weren't passionate about my workshop. But they were clearly passionate about birds.

JONATHAN TOM Passion is vital, because passion-driven people get things done. The foundation to volunteer leadership is passion. Recruiting, motivating, managing, and retaining volunteers begins with passion. It begins with *your* passion, and then what volunteers do depends on *their* passion. However, all of this passion needs to be focused like a laser beam. Because without the power of a focused mission, passion is rendered impotent.

Focus: The Power of Focused Mission

How did a bunch of passionate gym teachers and coaches—the people making up CASE—change legislation? The answer is in the difference between a laser beam and a lightbulb. These volunteers were united in their cause, and their focus was like a laser beam.

Lasers can burn through steel in a matter of seconds, while the most powerful lamp will have trouble even making steel warm. The difference between the laser and light is solidarity. In a laser, a photon moves along and invites another photon to join him on his voyage. Then, these two photons invite two more photons to join the group. Soon there is a huge army of photons marching in step with each other. This unity gives the laser its power. A lightbulb might have just as many photons, but each goes its own independent way, sometimes even disrupting other photons. As a result, much of a bulb's power is wasted and can't be forced to do any useful work. The laser, because of its unity, is like an army marching in tight formation, able to focus all of its power on its objective.

TOM The CASE volunteers clearly defined their focus: "Develop and pass a graduated license program so that 16-year-olds can't get a regular driver's license until they're 18." When they united with this single purpose, they won 90 percent of the battle. Every volunteer focused on that cause.

As I worked with them to brainstorm ways to accomplish their goal, they decided that they needed to partner with organizations and agencies that held power and money. So they recruited influential members of insurance companies—talk about money and power—and representatives from the Department of Motor Vehicles, who were also concerned about the problems of teenage drivers.

JONATHAN TOM The law passed on July 1, 1998, and was upgraded in 2006. In just over two years, the state developed a graduated driver's licensee program requiring teenage drivers to hold a provisional driver's license until they're 18. For the first six months, no passengers under age 20 can be in the car unless a licensed driver 25 or older is also present. For the first 12 months, no driving is permitted between midnight and 5 a.m. unless a licensed driver 25 or older is in the car. These laws changed all because of the focused laser-beam intensity of a small group of volunteers.

Unlike this group of volunteers, some volunteer teams aren't effective because they don't have a unified focus.

The key is focus. Without it, you're just a 60-watt bathroom bulb.

Focusing the new breed of volunteer. As a volunteer leader, how can you focus the energy of empowered volunteers who all want to do it their way? The new breed of volunteers is independent. In the 20th century, we used the metaphor of turning a huge battleship to illustrate leadership of an organization. All members of the organization were aboard the same ship going the same direction, with the leader at the helm. In the 21st century, we've had to change the metaphor. Now we talk about leading a school of empowered minnows. Volunteers are like empowered minnows, and each wants to swim its own direction. When the minnows are passionate about their beliefs, causes, or agendas, the only thing that can mobilize them is a unifying cause. This is where passion meets focus. The unified mission gets all the independent minnows thinking and acting in harmony.

Strategic Thinking: Keys for Mobilizing Passion

A cause can bring almost any team together. But how can you use your cause to mobilize your team? Think for a moment about the words that most of us learned in grade school:

We the People of the United States, in Order to form a more perfect Union, establish Justice, insure domestic Tranquility, provide for the common defense, promote the general Welfare, and secure the Blessings of Liberty for ourselves and our Prosperity, do ordain and establish this Constitution for the United States of America.

Why has this document become so revered? How has it lasted through incredible times of difficulty and change? It clearly lays out the fledgling government's purpose and mission. Thirteen independent states—loosely connected in a confederation, fragmented and bickering—found unity and direction in these opening words of the Constitution. In the same way, organizations need to clearly focus their dreams. As a volunteer leader, you can do that by focusing your organization's mission and vision. Let's look at each of these.

Mission. Look at your organization's mission statement. Does it excite the passion of your volunteers? Is it a rallying point for your organization? Does it communicate your cause? Does it state why you exist?

Look at these examples:

- *Habitat for Humanity®:* "Seeking to put God's love into action, Habitat for Humanity brings people together to build homes, communities and hope."[49]

- *Girl Scouts®:* "Girl Scouting builds girls of courage, confidence, and character, who make the world a better place!"[50]

- *PRIDE Industries:* "Create Jobs for People With Disabilities"[51]

A mission statement is absolutely essential for recruiting. You're not recruiting volunteers for jobs, but to complete specific tasks that fulfill your organization's mission. When volunteers believe that they're making a difference, they'll get into action. That's half the battle.

To write a mission statement, or affirm an existing mission statement, ask these questions:

1. Who are we?

2. What do we do?

3. Who do we serve? (Who are our members? Who are our customers? Who benefits from what we do?)

4. What benefit (service, impact) do we provide for those we serve?

5. Why are we unique? (Why are we better at what we do than any other organization or group?)

Answer each of those questions in 10 words or less. Then use those answers to write a one- or two-sentence mission statement.

You can use this simple process to help you focus the passion for your organization's unified mission. If people within your organization fight over the mission, you'll accomplish nothing. Certainly, you won't be able to attract the volunteers you need to accomplish anything. But when you become unified behind your mission, you can change the world!

Vision. In addition to a strong mission statement, leaders can use an energizing vision statement to focus passion.

TOM What's the difference between a mission statement and a vision statement? I faced this question recently when I had the opportunity to facilitate a strategic plan with 12 leaders of an organization. In preparation, I researched the difference. When I did an online search of the question through Google, I got 6,300,000 answers. I especially enjoyed the satirical definition from the mind of Tom Terez, coordinator of the Meaning At Work Project. He claims:

A mission statement contains two semicolons, two dashes, and at least two business words, while a vision statement contains only one dash, but makes up for it with at least one run-on sentence.[52]

 So what is a vision statement? Although five authors will give five different answers, we define the mission and vision statements as follows:

- A *mission statement* states your cause. It states why you exist and the service you provide for the people you serve.

- A *vision statement* states your future. It declares where you want to go. A vision statement is strategic—it puts strategic legs on the mission statement to capture the energy of your volunteers.

In *Built to Last*, Jim Collins and Jerry Porras call these statements BHAGs—Big Hairy Audacious Goals. Two of their BHAG examples are the space race and the Ford Motor Co.

- *Space race:* That this Nation should commit itself to achieving the goal, before this decade is out, of landing a man on the moon, and returning him safely to earth (John F. Kennedy, May 25, 1961).[53]

- *Ford Motor Co.:* To build a motor car for the great multitude... It will be so low in price that no man making a good salary will be unable to own one—and enjoy with his family the blessing of hours of pleasure in God's great open spaces...Everybody will be able to afford one, and everyone will have one. The horse will have disappeared from our highways, the automobile will be taken for granted (Henry Ford, 1907).[54]

As you develop mission and vision statements (or evaluate existing ones) for your organization, here are some important things to remember:

- Involve people from all areas and levels of the organization. They're the ones who'll be carrying out your mission and vision.

- Mission statements should focus your cause. They answer the question, "Why do we exist?"

- Vision statements project your future in wild ideas. They're outrageous (or BHAG) goals. A focused vision engages people—it reaches out and grabs people in the gut or heart. It's tangible, energizing, and highly focused. People should get it right away.

For additional help with mission and vision statements, go to "Strategic Planning Retreat—Agenda of Questions." This resource will help you think and plan strategically. Members of the California Association of Safety Educators used this tool to focus their passion and accomplish their mission and vision of changing California law to require graduated driver's licenses.

Community: Building Team Spirit

In addition to developing strong mission and vision statements, building community is an effective way to create and restore passion. Sometimes board members and volunteers become victims of one of the four passion robbers: fatigue, frustration, lack of fulfillment, or boredom.

JONATHAN A few years ago at a Source for Youth Ministry board meeting, the meeting was living up to its name. Everyone was truly "bored." It wasn't just the huge pile of logistical garbage we had to wade through; we were also tired and discouraged. Funds were tight and morale was low. As I looked around the table, our faces were all saying the same thing. "I'm here at this meeting because I have to be here."

We'd lost our passion.

After about 30 minutes of depressing reports, I stepped in and said, "I think we need to put aside our agenda tonight and do something else." Then I asked each board member to tell why he or she got involved with our organization in the first place. One by one, they told stories of how they watched God open the doors for our ministry. They shared about their excitement for what the ministry accomplishes each day, and the hundreds of thousands of kids' lives that God changes through the ministry.

Something miraculous occurred as we told our stories to each other. It was like asking a couple who's been married for many years to tell you the story of how they first met and fell in love. We were personally reinspired. Although we'd been working together for years, many of us had never heard these stories. Some of the stories were very personal, moving, and humorous. We gained a deeper respect for each other. But most of all, we were reminded of the validity of our cause. We gained renewed energy and passion for the menial tasks that were on the table. We were reminded of just how important the work of the organization was. And all of this only took about an hour.

JONATHAN TOM We recommend this exercise as an opener at a board retreat. It doesn't need to take long. A good leader or facilitator can keep it moving along. Without making a big deal of it, your board will be quickly re-energized and connected.

Some volunteer managers think that community will just happen if volunteers spend time working together. While that can occur, leaders know that you can't leave community building to chance. It has to be intentional.

One way to build community is to do team-building activities together and to go on community-enhancing retreats. Start off meetings with icebreakers—games that encourage participants to reveal something personal about themselves or that help participants get to know each other personally. The idea is more than just having fun. Icebreakers help create community because they build on trust and understanding.

For icebreakers that you can use to help intentionally build community with your volunteer leaders, go to "Icebreakers and Openers" on page 258.

Be careful the "urgent tasks" your organization faces don't replace community building. Community is essential for creating or restoring passion.

Training and Development: A Valuable Tool for Instilling Passion

Training volunteers is touchy. The new breed of volunteers often consists of professionals who've already received a lot of training in leadership and management. Some will groan when you mention training and development: "I've had to endure enough of these training seminars at my job. Do I have to endure them here, too?" The last thing they want is to attend another training seminar.

Yet as a volunteer leader, you'll naturally want to be a teacher, mentor, on-the-job trainer, and developer of personnel. You'll make training and development a priority because when volunteers understand your organization's mission, vision, and desired outcomes, they'll be even more passionate about what they do.

Give training a context. Putting training and development into context is a good way to get over the resistance of volunteers. A context means giving all volunteers the same grid to work from. If they understand the context, then they don't need a list of rules.

Chris Radloff, from Camp Timber-lee, says that training is one of his most important roles as a leader. He has one of the most effective training programs for volunteers that we've ever seen. Chris believes in empowering his volunteers, and he believes that you empower volunteers by creating decision makers.

This avoids lists of rules. Volunteers at Timber-lee don't have to be told, "Don't throw mud at kids." Instead, they can ask themselves, "How would throwing mud at kids help us with our mission or what we're trying to accomplish with campers?" The simple answer is, "It wouldn't help." So they don't do it. Chris calls this the Abraham Lincoln method of training. He explains:

Abraham Lincoln said something like, "Give me six hours to chop down a tree, and I'll spend the first four sharpening the axe." So that's why I spend most of my training reinforcing desired outcomes—what we hope to accomplish with our campers. In a one-hour training, I'll spend 45 minutes on our desired outcomes. If our volunteers understand and buy in to the outcomes we desire, I'm helping them be decision makers. And creating decision makers is my No. 1 task of training.

Chris described a situation where one of the camp's female volunteers was counseling a cabin of girls who were "a bunch of spoiled snobs." They were way too worried about their appearance, and it was interfering with building meaningful relationships—one of the desired outcomes at Timber-lee. So at dinner, the counselor told the girls, "No silverware tonight." It was spaghetti night.

Imagine a 16-year-old in a Neiman Marcus sweater shoving spaghetti in her face with her hands. To an outside observer, this might seem crude. But those girls were finally having fun, and the volunteer was achieving three of Camp Timber-lee's desired outcomes at this dinner: providing a learning experience, building significant memories, and breaking down the walls that pave the way to meaningful relationships.

Something else was going on two tables over that might have appeared contradictory to the outside observer. One of the camp's male counselors had a bunch of freshman guys that were acting rude, unkempt, and abrasive. On this particular night—spaghetti night—he made his guys shower, dress up, and eat a proper dinner, using the appropriate silverware. Two totally different tables, using totally different methodology—yet both were achieving the exact same desired outcomes.

If Chris had just told his staff, "Hey, make sure your kids eat properly, because we've always done it that way!" his volunteers would have missed opportunities like this.

What we like about Chris' approach is that he gives training a context—it directly relates to how he wants his volunteer counselors to make decisions. He wants to empower them, and he does it by focusing on and teaching them about the importance of accomplishing the camp's objectives.

Use role-playing. This is another great training tool that helps volunteers understand your cause and feel empowered to make decisions on their own.

TOM When I was a sophomore in college, I got a job at the university information desk. Each day when I showed up at work, Miss Rees, my supervisor, role-played with me.

She took me aside and said, "Ring, ring."

I picked up an imaginary phone and answered, "Information Desk."

Then she asked a question to see how I'd answer. I'll never forget my first day on the job. She said, "Ring, ring." (OK, that part was pretty irritating.)

I answered, "Information Desk."

Then she said, "I have a dead alligator that I'd like to donate to the school. Are you interested in it?"

I was speechless. As a college sophomore, I thought I knew everything. I was about to say, "No, we don't want it," but I thought I should ask Miss Rees.

She said, "Think, Tom, who in the school would like a dead alligator?"

I guessed, "The science department?"

She pushed me harder and said, "Come on, Tom; think. Who in the science department might be able to use a dead alligator? Did you ever dissect dead frogs and worms in high school?"

I was a little slow my first day. But I finally got it and responded on my imaginary phone, "One minute, please. I'll transfer your call to the biology department."

Each day, Miss Rees spent the first five minutes of my work shift with these role-plays. It got to be a fun challenge to see if she could come up with a question that I couldn't answer.

JONATHAN **TOM** *Use mentors and video replay.* Docents at the California State Railroad Museum each complete 80 hours of training. This training is essential because when visitors enter the museum, the only people they have contact with are the docents, who serve as tour guides. During the training, docents must prepare a 10-minute talk three times in front of their peers. The last talk is videotaped for feedback. This is a fantastic way for them to develop their presentation skills.

After the docents graduate from the training, they have mentors for another six months. You might think this sounds a little severe. But if you ever visit the museum, take note of the caliber of volunteers.

Use staff meetings. Staff meetings provide a great time to practice "continuing education" to keep volunteers sharp.

JONATHAN Awhile back, I was in Los Angeles visiting my friend Brian, a sergeant in the Los Angeles Police Department. Brian asked if I wanted to go on a "ride along," and I gladly accepted.

So there I was—in the heart of Los Angeles, in the middle of the night, riding shotgun in a police car. (Brian had to keep telling me to stop playing with the lights and siren!) I loved the experience. But the evening didn't begin by jumping in a car. It all started with roll call.

All the police from that shift gathered together in a room before they headed out to the streets. During this 20-minute meeting, about 15 minutes of it was continuing education.

One officer shared an experience that two officers had the previous day. A fight had been reported in the street. When officers arrived on the scene, a trail of blood led to the door of the house, with blood also on the doorknob. The two officers had knocked on the door, but no one answered.

So the sergeant running the training asked, "Can we enter?" Officers from around the room started answering. They discussed "probable cause." The sergeant gradually revealed other details. The consensus in the room was, "Yes, enter the house."

The trainer said, "That's what we did." Then, on a whiteboard, he drew the interior layout of the house, drawing X's where people were sitting on a couch.

"What now?" he asked.

People from around the room shouted out answers: "Ask to see their hands."

"We did." Then he circled an X on the couch. "But this guy wasn't moving at all." Then he drew another X on the couch, and said, "When officers looked closer, they noticed a 3-year-old kid sleeping right here next to the man."

"Now what?" he asked.

The discussion in the room was intense, because the situation wasn't just made up in someone's mind. It had just occurred the day before. And the more the officers got into it, the more the trainer disclosed about the situation.

This was a real-life experience turned into a teaching opportunity. The officers were able to objectively evaluate the good and the bad in the situation. Most importantly, they assessed what could be done better next time.

As we rolled out of that meeting, I asked Brian how often they did these training sessions. His answer: "Every day."

For an example of using a teachable moment for training during a staff meeting, go to "The Volunteer Manager's Meeting" in Chapter 10.

Use case studies. Another great training method that volunteer leaders can use to open up discussion and keep passion alive among volunteers is the case study.

You can easily create your own case studies. Don't let writing these scare you. Simply come up with a situation where some things go wrong and some things go right. Make up characters and describe the interaction between the volunteer manager and volunteers. Include discussion questions such as these:

- What went wrong? Find as many things that went wrong as possible.

- How could the situation have been avoided?

- What can be done now?

- What did [character] do right in this situation?

- What did [character] do wrong in this situation?

- What do you see about our organization that we can learn from this example?

We usually add one more question that might focus on the whole point of the case study such as, "How can you be sure that when you hand off a project to a volunteer team member that they won't drop the ball?"

We like to have participants read the case study and then discuss the questions in small groups. One person from each group can report the answers to the larger group. You can use the answers to teach important volunteer-management skills.

For examples of case studies, go to "Epilogue—A Leadership Case Study," on page 199. This case study presents one person doing things right. Also go to "Sample Training Exercise—A Case Study: 'Symptoms of Staff Resistance' " on page 269. This case study presents a situation where things go wrong.

Training is essential for your volunteers. But volunteer managers also need management training on recruiting, motivating, managing, empowering, and performance coaching—the topics covered in Chapters 1 through 8 of this book. Continue to sharpen your axe.

WHY THESE ESSENTIALS ARE...ESSENTIAL (DUH!)

Great volunteer teams consist of passionate people who have a focused vision, believe in their mission, and empower each other with their initiative and skill development. As a volunteer leader, ask yourself and your leadership team these questions:

1. Passion: Are our volunteers passionate about our mission? It all starts here.

2. Focus: Is that passion focused like a laser or unfocused like a lukewarm lightbulb?

3. Strategy: Are we thinking strategically, using carefully crafted mission and vision statements?

4. Team: How are we building community among our volunteers? Do they love working with us?

5. Training: Is our training geared for the new breed of volunteers who want to do it their way?

Volunteer Power

Do you want to move beyond just recruiting and leading volunteers? Do you want to unleash their power? When volunteer leaders learn how to mobilize volunteers to accomplish their passion, the volunteers can become so powerful that they can change laws, feed and house thousands of homeless people, or make a difference in the environment. In short, they can change lives forever!

This power isn't limited to highly paid executives with résumés as long as a roll of paper towels. This amazing power can be found in volunteers. But it will take your leadership to bring focus to their passion.

CHAPTER 10

EPILOGUE—A LEADERSHIP CASE STUDY

A Fable of How to Do It Right

HOW TO USE THIS CASE STUDY

Print copies of this case study and instruct your volunteer leaders to read it. (You have permission to reprint it.) As they read, encourage them to answer the following:

- What were your "Ahas"?

- What did you like the best?

- What did you see that our organization could be doing better?

- Look at the questions David answers on his ride home at the end of the story. How would you answer those questions?

The following story is the conclusion of "The Common Predicament" in the introduction to this book. Although the story is fictional, nothing in the story is untrue or unrealistic. Between the two of us, we have more than 70 years of volunteer leadership experience. We've either done what Alissa has done in this story or have witnessed other leaders in the nonprofit world who are like Alissa.

This story is spot on.

☝ *To review "The Common Predicament: Where It All Begins," go to page i.*

Part 1

NBA Cares

David came home after a hard day at the city youth center. Completely exhausted, he wondered how much longer he could keep going. When he accepted the job as executive director a few years earlier, he believed he'd finally fulfill his passion of working with inner-city kids. But tonight, he realized that he'd lost his passion. He was dry and ready to give up.

As he turned on the NBA game to escape his thoughts, he saw something that just made him feel worse. A similar youth center just an hour's drive away was featured on the NBA Cares segment. NBA players were painting, reading, working on computers, and having their pictures taken with volunteers and kids at this center. The final part of the story was an interview with the director of the center—a young woman named Alissa. She talked about their activities, the positive influence they were having in the community, and how much she appreciated the NBA players who spent the afternoon at the center.

The clincher for David came with the reporter's summary:

In the few years since Alissa became director of the center, it has become a thriving place that offers recreational opportunities and programs in the arts, education, health, culture, and an overall emphasis on the development of youth. Under Alissa's leadership, the center and its programs serve as a refuge for many of the youth who reside in neighborhoods where they're regularly exposed to violence and crime. More than 100 volunteers, many of whom put in at least four hours a week, help Alissa make her dream a reality. And she does this with only one other paid staff person. The center stands as a dynamic volunteer success story that the city is proud of.

David was devastated, certain that he'd failed. He'd arrived at his center the same time Alissa did. Yet all he had to show for his work was 10 volunteers who were getting tired and felt overworked. He had no other staff. He'd inherited a wonderful facility, but it was starting to show signs of age. He sure wished he could get the NBA to care about his mission.

As he wondered what to do, David hardly slept that night. But when he got up in the morning, he decided that he wouldn't accept failure. He'd try something he'd never done before. He'd always been able to figure things out himself, but today he'd ask for help. As soon as he got to his office, he called the center he'd seen on TV and asked for Alissa. The volunteer receptionist put him right through, and David found Alissa warm and engaging.

David explained his frustration to Alissa and asked if he could drop in, visit the center, and perhaps spend an hour with her to get some advice. "I feel like the Lone Ranger," David said. "It seems that I'm doing everything myself. I had a successful volunteer management experience 10 years ago, but something has changed. I don't know if it's me or the times or what. But I'm sinking, and I need to see someone who's doing it right."

"I agree," Alissa sympathized. "I've realized that the volunteer world is very different than it was even 10 years ago. Fortunately, I had a good mentor who helped me." Then she said something that surprised David. "I'd love to have you visit. But if you really want to get a good look at what we're doing, you should come next Monday morning around 11 and meet the volunteer in charge of our Monday activities. Bring a sack lunch with you because on that day the volunteers in charge of the Tuesday, Wednesday, and Thursday activities are coming in for a special meeting. We call these people our leadpersons. We're actually in the middle of recruiting someone to lead Friday's activities. After the meeting, you can hang around and watch our volunteers in action and ask any questions you want." David was ecstatic.

Alissa continued: "If you'd like, at 3 that afternoon, you and I can meet to debrief. Then you'll have an opportunity to clarify anything you have questions about."

David couldn't believe Alissa was so willing to help, and he couldn't resist asking, "Alissa, when the center is so successful—and you must be really busy—why are you willing to spend this time with me?"

Alissa's answer was inspiring. "Because I have a passion for kids— not just the kids in our city. And if our program can help other groups reach more kids, I'm excited to share." This was the best news David had heard in a year.

"And besides," Alissa added. "I really don't have anything to do. Our volunteers do everything, so I have tons of time to meet with you."

"Yeah, right!" David responded.

"OK, I'm joking," Alissa laughed. "But believe it or not, I'm not nearly as stressed or pressured as during my first year. I have great people who carry a lot of the load and actually run much of the program. I spend my time doing a lot of stuff other than just recruiting volunteers."

She had David's attention.

Part 2

Meeting Carl

When David arrived to meet Carl, the Monday volunteer leadperson, David was surprised. Carl was a 68-year-old retired Air Force lieutenant colonel. He'd also been a pilot for American Airlines for 20 years after retiring from the Air Force. He was warm and inviting, greeting David enthusiastically. "We're excited that you can join us for the day. Let me walk you through our facility."

As David and Carl walked through the center, David saw that the facility's basic layout was the same as his. One difference was that Alissa's center had recently started a boxing program and converted part of the gym to an impressive boxing facility. Carl explained that they'd found boxing to be a great way to reach some of the inner-city kids, and the discipline and training of the boxing program proved to be another effective way to accomplish their mission.

Carl added that the opportunity had opened up when Alissa made a presentation to the local Rotary club. Afterward, a former boxer in the Navy asked her if she'd ever consider starting a boxing program. Alissa jumped at the chance, and soon they had five active volunteer coaches training young boxers. One of the boxers might even go to the Olympics. David got excited as he thought of the possibilities back home, noticing that his center's facilities were just as good as this one.

"So how did you get involved in being a volunteer?" David asked.

"I saw a story in the paper about the center, called Alissa, and asked if I could help out," Carl responded. "She told me to drop by and gave me a tour. She asked me questions about my hobbies and interests. When she heard me talk about how I love to make model planes, she got an idea. She said one boy, a preteen, was very lonely and just needed a friend. She asked if I'd just drop by and meet the young man to see if there was a connection between us. This boy, Nathan, was artistic, and she wondered if he'd like to try building models with someone. So I purchased a model glider and brought it with me when I met Nathan. He and I really connected. One meeting, and I was hooked. One thing led to another and now we have a model club in the center, and the younger boys work on the models each week."

"How did you move from making models to being the Monday leadperson?" David asked. "In fact, what is a leadperson volunteer?"

"After a year, the model program began to grow, but I discovered that only a few of the boys wanted to do models. In fact, most of the boys were either interested in sports or video games. I didn't have a background in either of those, so I asked some of my friends to help out. They knew people who knew people—and the next thing I knew, I had five guys helping me. Most of them I know from my church. We just sort of fell into the Monday group because of our schedules and availability.

"Alissa noticed this, and one day asked if she could run an idea past me. She wondered if I would totally take charge of Monday and recruit and manage all of the activities on that day. She laughed and said her only concern was if I would run it like a military operation. She reminded me gently that this was a volunteer organization—not the Air Force. I understood her concern, but I was excited to give it a try.

"I've had this position for more than a year and a half now, and I have 10 volunteers. Each of my volunteers puts in at least four hours every Monday. I always have eight that are here each week. I have to be a bit flexible with the schedule, but so far it works great. Some are college students, some are mothers who come to the center when their kids are at school, and one is a dentist who takes a long lunch and comes in every Monday from 11:30 to 2.

"I also have a very energetic group of volunteers who are young single professionals. They do kind of an evening shift after their workday. I happened to get one young woman, Natasha, from a high-tech company, and she recruited three of her friends. Now that company has joined in partnership with the center and lists it as one of their 'giving back to the community' projects. Natasha has also brought in a lot of volunteers for other days. In fact, when some of the other leadpersons have a need for volunteers, they often call Natasha and she gives them some people to contact."

Carl looked at his watch and said, "Wow, we've got to get to our meeting. Alissa always starts her meetings on time."

Carl led David to the break room where they grabbed their sack lunches before heading to the conference room for the volunteer managers meeting. The break room was a special room just for volunteers. Dave noticed that it had schedules on one wall and a bunch of pictures on the others. There was a refrigerator, a small microwave, and three very comfortable-looking couches.

Part 3

The Volunteer Managers Meeting

At noon, three other volunteers joined Carl and Alissa for their meeting. Alissa introduced David and gave a brief description of why he was attending their meeting. Then she introduced the three volunteers David hadn't met.

Dixie, a woman in her 40s with three almost-grown children, was a nurse who worked part time in the "burn ward" at a local hospital. She'd been volunteering at the center for two years.

John owned a successful auto repair shop. He took Tuesdays off to spend at the center. He had two passions—cars and kids. He was trying to see if he could somehow develop an auto-repair training program at the center but hadn't worked out all of the logistics.

Neil, a college professor in social services, started volunteering at the center to keep his perspective fresh about what he was teaching. But he became so excited about the center that he began to bring students with him to fulfill their volunteer requirements. He soon became the Wednesday leadperson and, so far, had been able to work his teaching schedule around his commitment at the center.

Alissa began, "The purpose of the meeting today is to choose a list of candidates to be a Friday leadperson and talk about the interview questions, so that we can set up interviews."

John joked to David, "We love that Alissa's meetings are focused and to the point. We get in and out fast because we know exactly what we're doing." David noticed that all of these volunteers respected Alissa's professionalism.

Carl and Dixie recommended people from their teams, and the group of leadpersons decided to set up two interviews.

That conversation took just seven minutes. Then Alissa did what seemed strange to David. She took a half-hour and did a training session on interview techniques. She taught the group how to ask behavior-based questions instead of hypothetical questions. She explained how they could frame questions to focus on past volunteer experience instead of asking "What if" questions.

She gave some examples:

1. Tell me about your experience in recruiting a volunteer for a specific position.

2. Describe a time when working with a volunteer that you faced problems or stresses that tested your coping skills. What did you do?

3. Tell me about a time when you had to use your spoken communication skills in order to get an important point across to a volunteer.

Then she had the group members prepare questions and practice interviewing each other. She closed the meeting by determining several optional dates for the interview. The meeting was over in 45 minutes.

Part 4

The Walk-Around

David and Carl walked out into the center. Kids began showing up around 1:30, but all the volunteers had arrived at 1:15. Carl led a quick, stand-up, check-in meeting with his crew—eight volunteers that day. He explained that Joan had called in sick and Bill was out of town on a business trip. Someone pointed out that Joan had missed the last four weeks and wondered if she was OK. Carl noted it, expressed his own concern, and mentioned something about talking to Alissa. David made a mental note of the first question he wanted to ask Alissa: "When does the leadperson volunteer turn over follow-up to you?"

Volunteers each gave a one-minute report of the previous Monday's activities and what they had planned for this day. With that, the meeting ended and Carl took David around to see the volunteers in action.

Carl took David by the break room. "Since many of the volunteers spend four hours or more a day at the center, we encourage them to take a break just as if they were an employee." Carl pulled a Pepsi® out of the fridge and tossed David one without asking. David didn't mind. He liked Pepsi.

Carl continued. "I always stop in the break room to visit with volunteers. Alissa does, too, and frankly she's the one they want to see." Carl laughed. "They're honored when Alissa stops to visit with them, even if it's just small talk."

David asked Carl, "The meeting that you had today, do you do that often?"

Carl explained to David that today's gathering was their monthly meeting. They rarely met at noon, but did today because of trying to set up the interviews. Usually, they meet on the second Tuesday of the month at 6 p.m. Alissa orders pizza or sandwiches, as most people come directly from work. The meetings never last more than 90 minutes, and they're always to the point.

Carl continued explaining. "Every meeting has a specific focus. About once a quarter, Alissa spends the last 30 minutes of the meeting training us on some aspect of volunteer management." David made another mental note, "Ask about training and how Alissa finds training material for these professional leadpersons who've probably already heard it all."

David kept evaluating what he was seeing and comparing it to his own ministry. He didn't see anything he couldn't do based on facilities. And he didn't see anything that his center was lacking, except one thing: Alissa. David was realizing that everything happening in this center was because of Alissa's leadership. He couldn't wait to spend an hour with her and ask how she did it.

Part 5

The Debriefing

At 3 p.m., David thanked Carl for his time and went to Alissa's office. She was waiting with a stack of sample forms such as applications, agreements, and position charters. She handed them to David and then asked, "So what did you think?"

David just sat there for a moment, overwhelmed. He blinked a couple of times, sighing deeply. "I'm trying to process it. I think it'll be months before I really understand the impact of this day."

David leaned forward in his chair. "I can't thank you enough. I know your time is really valuable, so I jotted down several questions, if I can ask them?"

"Fire away," Alissa responded.

Discipline. David began, "One of the things I noticed at the pre-shift huddle with Carl is that someone named Joan hadn't been here for four weeks. Everyone seemed concerned. Carl said that she'd called in sick. And then he said that he'd asked you to talk to her. I was wondering how you decide who will talk to a person who begins not fulfilling his or her commitments?"

"Wow, you're good!" Alissa said, smiling. "I'm glad you caught that, because it's an important part of keeping volunteers, and I take volunteer retention very seriously. When we allow volunteers to go back on their commitments, it discourages the faithful volunteers. It lowers the bar and they begin not taking their roles very seriously.

When volunteers don't take it seriously, you begin a slippery slope that can kill the whole volunteer program.

"So when that happens," Alissa continued, "I step in. I call it performance coaching. It's not easy, so I take on that responsibility."

"What do you do?"

Alissa crossed her arms and leaned back in her chair. "This is our procedure: When a volunteer misses, the leadperson contacts him or her a few times to make sure everything's OK. We want to be sure there isn't a family emergency, sickness, or something else. The leadperson can do that well. I do ask the leadperson to document the talk, stating the area of commitment the volunteer isn't keeping. But if behavior doesn't change, I set up an appointment with the person to talk about it. I'm pretty firm, stating our policy and how it lets the whole team down—and lets the kids down—when the volunteers don't show. If I find out it's a personal problem, I suggest taking a breather for a few months. I call it a sabbatical. In some cases, I just suggest that if the volunteer can't keep the commitment, it'd be best for everyone if they resigned until they can.

"Of course, this isn't easy. But I don't want to lose my leadpersons, so I take care of it. I also follow labor laws to make sure that we don't have a lawsuit."

"Have you ever had to fire anyone?" David asked.

"Sure, but I wouldn't call it 'firing,' " Alissa responded. "I've found that because we do a thorough job during interviews to set standards, when volunteers can't keep their commitments, they're relieved to take a break."

Staff. "That leads to my next question. Tell me about your paid staff," David questioned.

Alissa gleamed. "I'm proud of my one staff member: Margie. She was the greatest find, and I don't think we'd be where we are today without her."

"What does she do and how did you find her?" David asked.

"Margie is our director of admin volunteers," Alissa said. "In other words, she's our office manager. But when I recruited her, I spent most of the time asking her about her volunteer experience. Her husband is retired Army, and she worked civil service on the base and also led many volunteer programs for Army wives and families. She's set up the whole office staff. We have five women who each spend four hours a week in our office doing office tasks, we have one off-site volunteer who does all the layout work for our printing, and we have a volunteer Web master who's also off-site—out of state, actually. Margie recruited most of them and now manages their work.

"Twice a year, we do a special luncheon for our office staff, and we also send them to special training. Everyone goes except the out-of-state Web master. They love it. For example, we've paid to upgrade their office skills to become Microsoft® -certified. In exchange, they commit to at least two years with us. Most have stayed on longer. Some haven't worked outside the home while raising their children. But now their children are headed to college, so they've used this opportunity to upgrade their skills to get back into the job market. Some of our volunteers have gotten super jobs. It's a real win/win."

Training. "Speaking of training, that's another question I have," David said. "Today, you used the last 30 minutes of your staff meeting for training on interview skills. What other things do you train volunteers on?"

Alissa shared, "I work hard on training. I might copy an article in a volunteer magazine and pass it around to discuss. I might show a short training DVD, and we discuss it. We do a lot of role-play. I'll bring up something that really took place in the center or a phone call that came in, and ask volunteers to role-play how they'd handle each situation."

Boards. Then David asked a question he'd been curious about since the previous Friday night. "How on earth did you get NBA players to come and paint your facility? That must have given you great credibility and publicity that you could never buy. How did you do it?"

Alissa grinned as she answered, "Wasn't that awesome? That was huge. And the best part was that our all of our volunteers showed up and got their pictures taken with an NBA star. Cool perk. But you asked how I got them to come. I didn't. One of our board members had that contact. You know the four W's of boards?"

David asked, "The what?"

Alissa repeated, "The four W's. You always need four W's on your board of directors." Alissa held up her hand and counted on her fingers as she named them off. "I learned years ago to look for wealth, weight, wisdom, or worker. People who are *wealthy* know other people who are wealthy who can give you the money you need. One of my mottos is 'No Money, No Mission.' I need board members who can give and raise funds. Second, board members who have *weight* in the community can open all kinds of doors. One of our board members is a personal friend with the owner of our NBA team, and they were looking for a place to give back to the community. He arranged the project for NBA Cares. Third, *wise* board members are able to set policies that empower me to do my job.

"The last one, I don't look for. I have found that wealthy and wise people who have influence are usually also workers. I don't expect a lot of meetings from my board members. We meet just three times a year to evaluate if we're accomplishing our mission, to hold us financially accountable, and to raise more money. I couldn't do what

I do without the board I have. When I have an opening on the board, I ask myself, 'Do I need more wealth, weight, or wisdom?' And I look for that kind of board member."

David thought, *And I bet they feel that they couldn't accomplish what they do without you.*

Leadership. David said, "I know we only have 10 minutes left. Talk to me about your leadership. You seem perfect. Don't you ever make mistakes? You've done more in a few years than many do in a lifetime. What's your secret?"

Alissa didn't even think before responding. "David, I learned through trial and error. I've made so many mistakes. In my first job as the leader of a nonprofit organization, I struggled the first few years. Then I learned that I needed to be intentional about my leadership.

"The first thing I did, which I continue to practice today, is take care of myself. I can't do this alone, and I need to make sure I'm not always just giving out. So I'm part of a support group of fellow strugglers who want to be winners. We're all executive directors of volunteer organizations, and we meet once a month for lunch. We share our struggles and help each other out. Once a year, we rent a cabin and spend two days together, like a retreat. Each of us writes a paper on a new trend or movement happening in the volunteer world. Then we discuss the papers. This is huge for me.

"Second, I read all I can on volunteer leadership. I subscribe to several e-zines and read constantly. Many provide similar information, but I always learn something, get a new idea, or think of something I should be doing that I'm not.

"I also always try to attend one conference a year. My leadership ability turned around when I started a continuing program of self-improvement."

David interrupted. "You said you're intentional about your leadership. Does that just mean being intentional about going to conferences, reading, and all this other stuff?"

"That's part of it," Alissa answered. "As I take care of my own personal development, I follow four steps of intentional leadership. First, I make sure we're focused on our mission.

"Second, as a leader I try to think strategically by creating personal and organizational vision. Every year, I set measurable goals. This year, I wanted to raise another $100,000 so we could start teaching young people technical skills such as computer skills, auto mechanics—that's John's dream—language arts, and so on. And I want to recruit two more leadpersons. Every six months I ask myself this question: 'What are 20 things I could be doing to better do our mission?' Then I spend an hour answering that question. Most of my 20 ideas aren't very good, but one or two of them are often wonderful. That's how I came up with the idea of a leadperson for each day. I'd been watching Carl, and I thought, 'He could be doing what I'm doing, and I think he would.'

"Third, I believe that leaders must intentionally build community. Visionaries often forget this part of leadership. But I work hard on spending relational time with our volunteers. I read all sorts of stuff on community-building activities so that we can have fun while we work.

"And finally, I'm committed to training. I read that Andy Grove, when he was the CEO of Intel, and Jack Welch, when he was the CEO of General Electric, both spent significant time training their leadership. I do the same."

David didn't want to overextend his welcome, so he thanked Alissa and invited her to drop by his center. Secretly, he hoped she wouldn't come too soon. Maybe in a year when he'd put some of these ideas in practice.

Part 6

The Drive Home

As David drove home, he stopped at a restaurant and looked at his notes. He'd learned more in one afternoon than in more than 20 years of volunteer experience or training. He also realized that he was dealing with a new breed of volunteers—a 21st century volunteer who was in some ways the same, but just different enough to make him shift the way he managed and led volunteers.

David was realizing that volunteer management is more leading than managing. David thought—mission, vision, community, and training. He sat at the restaurant for an hour as he started writing answers to these questions:

- What's our mission?

- What's our vision?

- How am I building community?

- How am I training my volunteer team?

The answers both bothered him and excited him. He had a new vision. He had a new passion. Then he ordered another round of coffee and wrote: "What 20 things could I be doing now to better do our mission?"

It was a long night.

Ten months later Alissa stopped by for a visit, and David wasn't embarrassed at all.

SECTION FOUR

RESOURCES

Why reinvent the wheel if it works? The following resources all work—we know because we use them. You can download them free at group.com/bonus and adapt them for your own organization.

Sample Position Charter

Sample Youth Ministry Volunteer Expectations

Sample Project Charter

Sample Youth Ministry Volunteer Application

Interview Guide for Hiring a Paid Volunteer Manager

Sample Youth Ministry Reference Form

Sample Questionnaire for Virtual Volunteers

Sample Board Code of Conduct

Strategic Planning Retreat—Agenda of Questions

SWOT Analysis Form

Icebreakers and Openers

Team-Building Activities

Sample Training Exercise—A Case Study: "Symptoms of Staff Resistance"

SAMPLE POSITION CHARTER

Effective recruiting demands a clear, complete, and brief presentation of a volunteer position's roles and responsibilities. The most effective way to begin this process is to develop a position charter.

The following two-step process provides a simple way to develop a complete and mission-driven position charter.

Step 1

The first step is to develop the objective, or mission, for the position. Use the following five questions to develop the objective. The following is a sample from the volunteer receptionist for the ABC Adult Day Care Center. Sample answers are in italics.

1. What's the position? *Receptionist for ABC Adult Care Center.*

2. What are the duties? *Answer the phone, take messages, distribute mail, make coffee, and buy doughnuts.*

3. What's unique about the person in this position? *An enthusiastic and positive person, with great telephone voice and skills. Loves people and has a knack for details. Gets phone messages correct.*

4. What value does this position contribute to the mission of the organization? (What are the benefits of this job to customers?) *Customers feel great when they finish talking on the phone with ABC Adult Care Center. They have the confidence that their messages are going to be delivered. The office is always warm, friendly, and neat for all internal and external customers, which also makes it a fun place to work.*

5. Who are the customers? *Internal: Staff members. The receptionist seeks to serve staff by delivering correct messages and making the office a fun place to work. The receptionist should have a friendly and positive greeting as each person comes in the door. External: All current and prospective clients. The receptionist seeks to know them all, keep up on their current business needs, keep records of what they need, and make sure that requests are directed to the correct staff member.*

Put these answers together in a few-sentence objective statement for the position. Start the statement with the words, "To contribute to the patient care of ABC Adult Day Care Center by..." An example for this position follows:

Position Objective: *To contribute to the quality patient care of ABC Adult Care Center by assuming the primary responsibility for front-line contact with every vender, customer, and employee. The receptionist will accomplish this by building confidence and trust with each person who calls or visits ABC Care Center, communicating to all internal and external customers how important they are to us, and that we value their service. The receptionist will seek to build a trusting relationship with each patient, vendor, customer, and employee to ensure long-term satisfaction and to optimize the chances of add-on business and of the positive referral of new business to ABC Adult Care Center.*

Step 2

After you've written the position objective, outline the roles and responsibilities of the position. The following categories can help you develop these. Here are sample roles and responsibilities for the volunteer receptionist for ABC Adult Day Care Center. Sample answers are in italics.

Position Title: *Volunteer Receptionist*

Responsible to: *Administrator*

Key Objective: *To contribute to the quality patient care of ABC Adult Care Center by assuming the primary responsibility for front-line contact with every vender, customer, and employee. The receptionist will accomplish this by building confidence and trust with each person who calls or visits ABC Care Center, communicating to all internal and external customers how important they are to us, and that we value their service. The receptionist will seek to build a trusting relationship with each patient, vendor, customer, and employee to ensure long-term satisfaction and to optimize the chances of add-on business and of the positive referral of new business to ABC Adult Care Center.*

General Duties (same for all volunteers):

1. *Attend all volunteer staff meetings*

2. *Fill out weekly staff report*

3. *Turn in expense vouchers*

4. *Coordinate schedule with supervisor*

Specific Duties for This Position

Greeting

1. *Be at the receptionist desk 15 minutes early for a once-a-week, four-hour volunteer shift*

2. *Greet visitors, staff members, and volunteers as they enter the building*

3. *Offer visitors a cup of coffee*

4. *Seek to help visitors by answering questions and directing them toward their desired needs*

5. *Have all visitors sign guest log*

Answer the phone

1. *Answer before the third ring*

2. *Take messages—always writing down the phone number*

3. *Set up priority for answering the phone (who answers when the receptionist is on the phone?)*

4. *Set up system of delivering phone messages*

5. *Monitor the voice mail system*

Filing and mail

1. *Update all files*

2. *Open mail and distribute*

3. *Record and file all receipts for volunteer expenditures*

Coffee time

1. *Prepare conference room for volunteer and staff 10 a.m. or 3 p.m. coffee break*

2. *Pick up "goodies" for breaks*

SAMPLE YOUTH MINISTRY VOLUNTEER EXPECTATIONS

JONATHAN This simple form was something I gave to volunteers interested in volunteering with the student ministry I led. It provided a glimpse of the ministry to help volunteers decide if it was where they wanted to serve. You might adapt it or create something similar for your own organization.

YOUTH MINISTRY VOLUNTEER EXPECTATIONS

This ministry has many different opportunities available to help make a difference in the lives of kids. We have short-term project teams, set-up teams, and "help" roles—usually for people that can only help during certain hours of the week. We also have a role that we call our "volunteer staff." This page lays out the expectations we have for these volunteers.

Members of our volunteer staff are people who commit to hanging out with kids regularly. This hanging out breaks down to three different times:

1. "One-on-one times" apart from youth group

2. Weekly youth group

3. Events and activities

I list these expectations for volunteer staff not so they can see the "rules" they must abide by, but so that they can evaluate and budget their time and energy effectively to include this ministry in their schedule. Prospective volunteer staff members also need to see what kind of time commitment and duties can be expected.

One unique thing about being on the volunteer staff is the nature of the work we do. Being with kids, praying with others, and doing recreational activities is exciting. At the end of a rough day or week, this ministry isn't another pressure or loathed time commitment; it's a time when you can put all else aside and allow God to work through you while doing something you enjoy.

1. "One-on-one" times

More than anything else, spending "one-on-one" time with kids is the most important thing we do. These kids are reaching for attention. They all want to be listened to, noticed, and appreciated. Many of these kids don't get any individual attention at home. They don't know what it is to be liked, heard, or cared about. We can help fill that void in their lives.

Each staff person needs to be in contact with kids weekly. Sometimes this might just be a phone call or a text to see how things are going or if they are coming to the next event. At least once a month, we need to see a kid outside of ministry events and activities. My hope would be that some staff could meet with kids weekly or every other week. These times include any activity with just one (sometimes two) kid(s). Staff members can take kids out for a milkshake, go shopping with them, stand in the DMV line with them—almost anywhere! Some kids that drive you nuts during youth group are wonderful in one-on-one settings because they are totally different away from their friends.

2. Weekly youth group

In order to provide more nights free, we have been holding our staff meetings and actual youth group on the same night. In addition, we have dinner together as a staff every once in a while on a Sunday night; it's a fun time to fellowship and plan ahead.

Youth group is from 7 to 8:30 p.m. every Wednesday. It is an important time to attract kids, bring them in, and have a chance to get to know them.

3. Events and activities

Trips to amusement parks, monthly events, ski retreats, camping, and other events and activities are not only free to staff members but are also an excellent time to spend major bonus hours with kids.

SAMPLE PROJECT CHARTER

A sample project charter for an "Increase Membership" Task Force

What Is a Project Charter?

A project charter provides an understandable framework for all participants. It might be written for a large volunteer project (a seasonal convention) or it might be designed to resolve a particular problem.

The project charter:

- Describes the scope of the project and the desired outcomes

- Identifies the authority and resources delegated to the project

- Defines participants and their roles and responsibilities

- Identifies the guidelines in which the project will operate

What's the Structure of a Project Charter?

The project typically consists of four primary sections:

1. Project identification and scope

2. Authority and resource needs

3. Project roles and responsibilities

4. Project structure and schedule

The following sample project charter is for a membership recruitment task force. The sample answers are in italics.

---

1. Project identification and scope

Project Name/Title: *Membership Recruitment Task Force*

Background/Introduction/Purpose: *In the past two years, membership has decreased 5 percent. This team is being called together to develop a strategy to increase member retention and to add 100 new members in the next two years.*

Scope Statement (expected results/desired outcomes): *The membership committee will develop a strategy and action plan to increase member retention and add at least 100 new members by June 2014.*

2. Authority and resources

Who has the authority to make decisions and allocate funds? *The committee has the authority to spend up to $5,000 for this project. The committee is empowered to do what it takes to get the task done (be creative).*

What personnel resources are needed (expertise on the project team)? *A consultant who is a specialist on membership retention and recruitment; one proactive member from each of the regional chapters (eight people); a marketing specialist from our membership (one person); a past president (one person); a team leader (one person). Total 11 team members, plus a consultant.*

What's the budget? *Determined at initial meeting—this team created the following budget at its first meeting.*

- *Consultant ($2,500)*

- *Marketing materials ($1,500/mailing)*

- *Meetings ($1,000)*

What time is needed? *Six months.*

3. Roles and responsibilities

Tasks to be performed (note how all begin with an action verb followed by an object, those responsible, and a checkpoint date):

1. *Present the problem of a decreasing membership to the team and have team members brainstorm ways to increase membership (at first meeting)*

2. *Research and select a consultant to work with committee (Tom, Mary, and Bill; by January 1)*

3. *Develop membership-calling campaign in each region (eight regional committee persons responsible; membership phone campaign in June)*

4. *Develop marketing materials (Tom; by April 1)*

5. *Mail out marketing materials to all present and past members (all committee members; in May)*

6. *Develop survey for members about why people join, leave, benefits, and so on (Bill, Joan, Jerri; by February 1)*

4. Project schedule

When the action steps are outlined from the brainstorming session, a timeline is developed.

- *January 15: Consultant retained*

- *February 10: Survey completed for approval*

- *March 1: Survey mailed out; rough draft of marketing material ready for approval*

- *April 1: Marketing material completed*

- *May 1: Mail out marketing materials*

- *June: Conduct phone campaign*

Observations about the project charter:

In this position charter, the scope of the charter is clear (increase membership by 100 members). The committee has a $10,000 budget to work with and a suggested outline of the people to pull into this project.

The method is wide-open. The committee is empowered, within those guidelines, to brainstorm and develop an effective plan. If committee members come up with a need for more resources (money, personnel), they can present their plan to the board for approval. The committee members need to develop their own plan and business processes (sections 3 and 4 of the project charter). In this way, the members of the committee own the solution to the problem.

YOUTH MINISTRY VOLUNTEER APPLICATION

Personal Information

Mr./Mrs./Ms: _____

Birth date: _____

Phone: _____

Address: _____

City: _____

Zip: _____

Spouse's Name (if applicable): _____

Occupation: _____

Children's Names & Ages (if applicable): _____

_____

_____

_____

Will your family/spouse support your involvement in this ministry? (please circle) Yes No

Education & Employment History

High School: _____

Year Graduated: _____

College: _____

Degree: _____

Date Completed: _____

Other: _____

Do you plan to pursue further education? (please circle) Yes No

Present Occupation: _____

Employer: _____

Address: _____

Phone: _____

Type of work/job title: _____

List types of work experience on this job: _____
_____
_____
_____
_____

Military Service: _____

Branch, Type of Discharge, Date _____
_____

Vehicle Information

Any traffic violations/accidents within the past 3 years? (please circle) Yes No

Do you own a car? (please circle) Yes No

Are you willing to drive for ministry functions? (please circle) Yes No

Church Background

Church currently attending: _____

List responsibilities or positions you have at church: _____

_____

_____

_____

Other organizations or programs you are involved in: _____

_____

_____

Describe your personal relationship with Jesus Christ: _____

_____

_____

_____

Have you led someone to faith in Christ? (please circle) Yes No

Describe the setting: _____

_____

_____

_____

Volunteer/Ministry Experience

Briefly describe your volunteer experience: _____
_____
_____
_____

How did you hear about volunteering for this ministry? _____
_____
_____

Why do you want to volunteer for this ministry? _____
_____
_____

What two greatest strengths do you bring to this ministry? _____
_____
_____

What are your two greatest weaknesses you feel may hinder your
ministry? _____
_____
_____

What training, other than what you have already mentioned, have you
had in Bible, theology, or counseling? _____
_____
_____

Ministry Interests

How many hours per week can you spend in this ministry?

(please circle) 2-4 4-6 6-8 8-10 10 or more

Have you been disciplined by a local church for anything that would hurt this ministry or tarnish the reputation of this ministry? (please circle) Yes No

If yes, please explain. _____

_____

_____

_____

_____

_____

Rate any of the following areas of student ministry you would like to help with (Leave blank if you have no interest in it):

1. I believe God has gifted me and I have a great vision for this service, ministry, or duty.

2. I'm interested or would like to grow in this service, ministry, or duty.

3. I am capable in this service, ministry, or duty, and will help out when needed.

____ Set-up and teardown of student ministry room

____ Media booth

____ Greeting students at the door

___ Event Security

___ MC (opening prayer, announcements, offering)

___ Games

___ Worship (singing or playing an instrument)

___ Jr. High camp

___ Speaking/teaching

___ Sr. High camp

___ Altar ministry (prayer)

___ "Church Days" representation

___ Girls' overnighters and similar events

___ Paintball

___ Girls' mentoring or small group discipleship

___ Birthday Bash (quarterly fun night)

___ Guys' overnighters and similar events

___ Amusement Park Day

___ Guys' mentoring or small group discipleship

___ Youth Convention

___ Jr. High/MidPoint Middle School Sunday class

___ Creative Arts/Drama

___ Sr. High/S4 (Supersonic Senior High Sunday School)

___ Evangelism/Outreach

___ Visitor ministry (cards to visitors, follow-up calls, so on)
___ Other_____

References

1. Name _____

Phone _____

Address _____

2. Name _____

Phone _____

Address _____

3. Name _____

Phone _____

Address _____

Confidential Background Information

Have you ever been convicted of a felony? (please circle) Yes No If
yes, please explain. _____

_____

_____

_____

Have you ever been formally accused of child abuse? (please circle)
Yes No If yes, please explain. _____

_____

_____

_____

Have you ever received psychiatric care that would affect your
relationship with our church? (please circle) Yes No If yes, please
explain. _____

_____

_____

_____

Responsibilities

I agree to allow you to do a background check (please circle) Yes No

Signature _____

Prayer Support

I agree to find three individuals committed to pray for me and for my ministry

1. Name _____

2. Name _____

3. Name _____

Signature _____

Statement of Faith

[place your church/organization's statement of faith here]

(please read and sign below)

I agree to this statement of faith. (please circle) Yes No

Waiver and Consent

I understand that by filling out this application, I waive any rights to confidentiality concerning the contents of this application. I authorize [CHURCH NAME] to contact the personal references I have identified and to conduct a reasonable investigation into my suitability for youth work. In signing this document, I also show that I subscribe wholeheartedly to the [CHURCH NAME] Statement of Faith as written above.

_____

Applicant's Signature   Date

INTERVIEW GUIDE FOR HIRING
A PAID VOLUNTEER MANAGER

The most important decision you make in managing volunteers is hiring your paid staff to supervise and manage volunteers. The following two steps will help you develop interview questions. We've included 10 sample behavior-based questions that you can modify for your situation, plus a sample interview outline.

Preparation for the Job Interview
Step 1: Identify the Needed Skills for the Position

Understand the position:

- What specific technical skills does the position involve?

- Does the position involve direct contact with organization members (customers)?

- With what departments does the position interact?

- Is there anything else important about this position?

Identify the technical skills the position requires (hard skills— measurable)

- Specific computer hardware and software

Identify the performance skills needed for the position (soft skills—difficult to measure)

- Managing

- Making presentations

- Making and being responsible for decisions

- Following established guidelines

- Following policies and procedures

- Dealing with other departments

- Dealing with the public

- Receiving an assignment and reporting its results when completed

Step 2: Develop specific behavior-based questions following these principles:

1. Avoid asking questions that can be answered "yes" or "no."

   - Avoid: "Do you like working with people?" "Did you like your last position?"

   - Ask instead: "Tell me your favorite thing about working with people." "What three things did you like most about your last position?"

2. Use open-ended questions that ask for specific examples of past volunteer experience. Try to avoid hypothetical questions about how the candidate might handle a future task.

3. Ask focused questions.

   - Not focused: "Tell me about your experience in working with volunteers."

   - Focused and behavior based: "Think back to when you were dealing with a high-maintenance volunteer. Tell me exactly how you handled that situation."

4. Ask behavior-based questions to determine the person's past behavior. Most people will perform exactly like they did in their last job. If they were late in their last position, they'll be late in this job. If they had a hard time working in teams in the last job, most likely they'll have a hard time working in teams in this position. Therefore, try to ask behavior-based questions that help you understand the prospective employee's past job performance.

   Avoid hypothetical questions about the future. Good interviewees love these questions because they can always say what they would do. However, you want to know what they have done.

Sample behavior-based questions:

   1. "Tell me about your previous experience working with volunteers and how you feel it prepares you for this staff position."

   2. "How have you handled volunteers who don't follow through?"

   3. "How have you increased your effectiveness with the work of volunteers?"

4. "Tell me about an exciting experience you have had in working side by side with a volunteer in your past work experience."

5. "Tell me about an unsuccessful experience you had in working with a volunteer in your last job."

6. "Describe a time in working with a volunteer when you were faced with problems or stresses that tested your coping skills. What did you do?"

7. "Tell me about a time when you had to use spoken communication skills in order to get a point across to a volunteer."

8. "Tell me about a job experience when you had to speak in order to be sure that the volunteer knew what you thought or felt."

9. "Give me an example of a time when you felt you were able to build motivation in your volunteer team."

10. "Give an example of a time when you had to use conflict resolution skills to solve a problem with volunteers."

YOUTH MINISTRY REFERENCE

Confidential Recommendation Form

TO BE COMPLETED BY APPLICANT:

Name of Applicant: _____

Name of Reference: _____

TO BE COMPLETED BY REFERENCE:

Our ministry would appreciate a confidential statement from you concerning the applicant named above evaluating his/her ability to undertake Christian ministry and his/her potential as a Christian leader. Please complete and return in the envelope provided.

Rate as follows:

Superior   Above Average   Average   Below Average   Don't Know

Kindness and generosity

Moral integrity

Patience

Perseverance

Self-discipline

Willingness to oppose injustice

Desire to serve God

Spiritual influence on others

Spiritual maturity

Theological insight

Completes assigned tasks

Leadership potential

Plans ahead

Punctuality

Wise use of money

Wise use of time

Working with others

Comments: _____

_____

_____

1. What are the applicant's greatest strengths? (Be as specific as
   possible) _____

   _____

   _____

   _____

2. Do you have any reason for lack of confidence in this applicant? (please circle) Yes No If yes, please explain: _____

_____

_____

_____

3. In your opinion, is the applicant able to be a positive role model to youth? _____

_____

_____

_____

Please indicate whether your recommendation is given:

_____ Enthusiastically _____ Strongly _____ Fairly Strongly
_____ Without Enthusiasm _____With Reluctance

OTHER REMARKS:

Signature: _____

Date: _____

Name: _____

Address: _____

Relationship to Applicant: _____

CONFIDENTIAL—Do not return to applicant. Please mail this statement directly to:

SAMPLE QUESTIONNAIRE FOR VIRTUAL VOLUNTEERS

As you interview potential virtual volunteers, you want to explore additional areas of volunteer responsibility that you wouldn't probe for face-to-face volunteers. The following is a sample outline of questions to ask potential virtual volunteers.

Organization philosophy

1. Why do you want to volunteer for our organization?

2. What about our mission excites you?

3. Tell about an experience you've had as a volunteer or staff member for an organization with a similar mission.

4. How did you hear about us?

Computer experience and equipment[55]

1. What kind of computer do you have?

2. Do you have a personal email account (home or work?)

3. Are you connected to the Internet, both via email and the Web?

4. Do you know how to use Web search engines? Which ones do you use regularly?

5. Do you know how to zip/unzip or stuff/unstuff a file?

6. Do you know how to email a document as an attachment?

7. What word processing software do you have? spreadsheet software?

8. How experienced are you with each of these software packages (such as database software, artwork software)? List the software packages your organization uses.

9. Do you know how to convert documents to other formats (such as one kind of word processing document to another? a word processing document to a spread sheet? one kind of database to another?)

10. Do you know how to import data into a database from another file?

11. Do you know how to export data from a database?

Self-motivation

1. Give me an example of a self-motivated project that you completed.

2. Tell me about a time that you had a project and how you organized your time to get it done.

3. Tell me about your weekly schedule and when you get your volunteer projects done.

4. Because most of our communication will be via email, send me an example of your writing skills and attention to detail.

(Many volunteer managers create a topic for the prospective volunteer to address in an email.)

5. Tell me about your workspace and how you handle or avoid distractions.

6. Tell me about your other commitments. Can you commit the _____ hours a week required for this volunteer assignment?

7. Tell me how you make sure that you answer each email in less than 48 hours (two working days).

SAMPLE BOARD CODE OF CONDUCT

If your organization has a policy against individual members of a board of directors for nonprofit organizations not receiving personal or business gain because of their position on the board (such as an insurance broker writing a huge policy because of his or her position on a board), you might want to institute a "code of conduct" that board members sign. The following is an example from the California Society of Association Executives.[56]

The Board expects of itself and its members ethical and business-like conduct. This commitment includes proper use of authority and appropriate decorum in group and individual behavior when acting as Board members.

- Board members must represent, with unconflicted loyalty, the interests of the membership. This accountability supersedes any conflicting loyalty such as that to advocacy or interest groups and membership on other Boards or staffs. This accountability supersedes the personal interests of any Board member acting as an individual consumer of the Society's services.

- Board members must avoid any conflict of interest with respect to their fiduciary responsibility.

- There must be no self-dealing or any conduct of private business or personal services between any Board members and the Society except as procedurally controlled to assure openness, competitive opportunity, and equal access to "inside" information.

- Board members must not use their positions to obtain for themselves, family members, or close associates, employment within the Society.

- Should a Board member be considered for employment by the Society, he or she must temporarily withdraw from Board deliberations, voting, and access to applicable Board information.

- Board members and members at large may not attempt to exercise individual authority over the Society or staff except as explicitly set forth in Board policies.

STRATEGIC PLANNING RETREAT

Agenda of Questions

A strategic planning retreat is a must for visionary boards. Use the following agenda of questions to facilitate a board through a vision retreat.

Introduction:

The ground rules during these days together include:

- Everyone should feel safe.

- There are no generals and privates at this retreat. Everyone shares as a genuine equal. Titles and positions are left at the door.

- We want to chase elephants, not rabbits. Anyone has the right to challenge the group if he or she feels the group is chasing rabbits. The group must then stop and vote without debate whether to continue that discussion.

- We want to keep the focus on our mission, not on private turf. Threatened people seldom make good decisions. We are in this together. To the degree possible, personal feeling should not impede the free exchange of information and opinion.

Discussion:

1. Where are we now?

The World We Face: The broad environmental analysis

- What is going on in the world today—politically, socially, economically, demographically, culturally, educationally?

- Will tomorrow's environment be different still?

- Can you give relevant statistics and information from media and other sources?

The World of [The Field Our Organization Is Within]

- What is happening in other like industries?

- What can we learn from their strengths and weaknesses?

- Who are the competitors in the field? What do we need to know about them?

Who Are We and Why Are We Here? Internal analysis

- SWOT analysis sheet—Strengths, Weaknesses, Opportunities, Threats

What Do We Value?

- What values have guided us to this present time?

- Do we still hold these values?

2. Why do we exist?

Focus Question: What is our mission?

Use these questions to help write a mission statement. Answer each of the questions in seven words or less:

- What are we?

- What do we do?

- Who are our customers/the people we are trying to reach?

- What is the benefit to our members?

- What makes us unique?

If you have a mission statement, affirm that statement.

3. Where do we want to be?

Our Vision for the Strategic Plan

Key questions:

- What is our vision for the future?

- What should be our focus for the coming years?

- What vision do we have for our organization in the next five years?

Criteria:

- Criteria should focus on vision—not process. (For example, the assembly line was a process—not a vision. Henry Ford's vision was to put a car in every garage. He developed the assembly line as a way to accomplish his vision.)

- Criteria are measurable.

Focus Question: Brainstorming exercise

What's our vision in the next year (two years)? Again, think vision—not process.

4. The Gap: How do we fill the gap between where we are and where we want to be?

Focus Questions:

- How wide is the gap between where we are and where we want to be?

- How do we measure that gap?

- What barriers keep us from reaching our vision?

- How can we bridge those barriers?

- What steps can we take to fill the gap?

Step One: Critical Success Factors

- Think of the goals to accomplish this mission

- Not the how, but the what (statements of hope)

- Necessary and sufficient rule: each is necessary and all are sufficient

- All must have "We must" or "We need"

- No less than four, and no more than eight

- Each should address a single issue (avoid the word "and")

- All must have a consensus; all must agree on what is vital to this mission

Step Two: Business processes to achieve these goals

- What are the business processes that we need to achieve each Critical Success Factor (goal)?

- What plans do we have to make?

- What people resources do we need?

- What financial resources do we need?

- Are any new structures necessary? If so, what are they?

For each critical success factor:

- Each should have an owner, the person responsible for carrying out the strategy.

- The owner should be a member of the board present at the meeting.

- Each success factor should begin with the words "we

must."

- No owner should have more than three or four strategies.

- Each should address a single issue.

- All must have consensus—all agree on what is vital to the mission.

5. Wrap up

Given who we are and what we represent, what could we do to establish this mission and attain these goals? Where do we go from here?

SWOT Analysis

In the boxes below, list in descending order of importance the three greatest strengths, weaknesses, opportunities, and threats facing our organization. As used here, *strengths* and *weaknesses* should refer to facts or behavior INSIDE the organization; *opportunities* and *threats* are used for factors OUTSIDE that affect our organization in some way. There are no right or wrong answers.

	STRENGTHS	WEAKNESSES
INTERNAL		
	OPPORTUNITIES	**THREATS**
EXTERNAL		

ICEBREAKERS AND OPENERS

These questions or activities will help you "break the ice" in meetings and planning events. Most of these give people an opportunity to share, listen to others, and get to know each other in a fun way.

Door-Opening Questions

Volunteers often don't really know much about each other at first. We can help by using a "disclosure" question to break down the masks that people often wear at meetings. When people get to know one another at a more personal level, they have more fun when working.

If this is a meeting of a dozen people or fewer, have everyone share the answers around the room. If you have a large group, divide everyone into groups of about six or eight.

Depending on the format, you may want to kick off your meeting with just one of these questions:

1. In high school you would most likely find me _____.
   Have each person fill in the blank.

Many of the answers we have heard include the following:

- In the bathroom smoking

- In the dean's office

- On the stage

- In the gym

- In the quad talking

2. What's the longest you've ever worn your hair? When?

3. What's the strangest food you've ever eaten?

4. What was your most prized toy as a child?

5. If you could have a T-shirt printed with a message, what would it say?

6. If you were stranded on a desert island:

   - What three items would you take with you?

   - What three people would you take with you?

7. If you discovered that you only had one year to live, what would you do differently?

8. Is there one thing you're not doing, that—if you did it—would have a great impact on your life?

9. If you could have one superhero power, what would it be and why?

10. If someone made a movie of your life, what actor/actress should probably play you?

These answers open the door for follow-up questions. Another variation of this icebreaker: Have people write down their answers on a 3x5 card. Collect the cards, shuffle them, and hand them out. Participants guess whose card they have.

Two Truths and a Lie

Participants say three things about themselves—two true and one a lie. Others guess which of the three statements is the lie.

This and That

Gather in a circle and select someone to begin, and then move clockwise around the circle. The first person says two similar items like pizza and ice cream (both foods). In three seconds or less, the second person has to say which of those two he likes better. If he beats the time limit, he gets to say two things to the next person. But if he doesn't make it, the next person says two items. Carry on with this game around the circle.

Highs and Lows

Participants share their high of the week and their low of the week. What experience is the best one of the week—your high? And what was the worst—your low?

My Favorite

Participants write down their answers to these questions:

- What is your favorite food?

- What website do you enjoy the most?

- What is your favorite TV show?

- What is your favorite hobby/pastime?

- What is the last album/song you bought/downloaded?

Participants sign their names and don't let anyone else see their answers. The leader then reads the answers to the whole group, and participants try to guess who each set of answers belongs to. Award a point for each correct guess. The person with the most points wins a prize.

Common Traits

Give participants a list of 5 to 10 traits that they must find in common with the people around them. For example: "Find someone who was born in the same month," "...someone who lives in your state," or "...someone who drives the same model of car." Participants with the most in common win a prize.

What Do We Have in Common?

Instruct participants to gather in groups of three. Their assignment for the next two minutes is to find five distinctive things that the three of them have in common. The three things cannot be job-related or obvious (such as all are women). Common items might include the following:

- All were born in the same state

- All are parents of three boys

- All drive a Toyota

Have the first groups that finish sit down. When the two minutes are up, tell the first three groups to introduce themselves and find out what they have in common.

The Hot Seat

Participants sit in a circle, and one by one, each takes the hot seat. The person in the "hot seat" has to answer a series of questions asked by another participant. Some sample questions:

- What were your greatest disappointments in the first third of your life? Second third? Recently?

- What was the greatest achievement you experienced before the 12th grade?

- What would you do if you won the lottery and received $1 million a year for the next 20 years?

- If you could have dinner with any person who has ever lived, who would you choose and why? What questions would you ask that person?

It's impossible to listen to the honest reflections of another team member without being drawn to that person.

Our Organization Can...

This opener can help set the stage for an event or planning weekend. Divide the room into four sections like a 40-yard football field (use blue masking tape, which doesn't leave a residue). Label the far left section *strongly agree*. Label the middle left section *agree*. Label the middle right section *disagree*. And finally label the far right section *strongly disagree*.

Now, make statements such as:

- "Our organization can change the world."

- "Our organization has a focused mission."

- "Our organization is facing a major threat."

- "Our organization is living in the past."

- "Our organization stands on the threshold of opportunity."

- "Our organization is alive and growing."

Come up with other statements unique to your organization. Have participants move to the part of the room matching their opinions. Once there, the people in that section should discuss why they chose their response. One member of each group can share with the larger group the consensus of why the individuals answered the way they did. Do this process with each statement.

Simple Lead-Ins

- Ask participants to state one or two "burning questions" they'd like answered in this session.

- Have participants describe one strategy/resource they've used successfully (relevant to the topic of the meeting/training).

- Have them state their personal definition of the topic (whether you're discussing the team, your community, your mission, a cause, or another topic).

The Check-In

Instruct each person to say, "I am _____ percent here today. The rest of me is [WHERE]." (They might say, "I am 40 percent here today. The rest of me is thinking about my family right now. We had a big fight last night.") Let each person talk about where his or her mind is. As a leader, you discover how big a job you have to get participants focused on your meeting agenda.

TEAM-BUILDING ACTIVITIES

Some of these simple activities can help teams learn to work together. But some of these involve much more (for example, "Building Interdependence" is a very serious exercise). Find more of these free ideas on TheSource4YM.com

---

Blind Square

This is a quick but effective team-building activity.

Supplies:

1. As many blindfolds as you have team members

2. One large rope, at least 40 feet in length

Simply blindfold all your team members and throw a rope on the ground next to them. Tell them to make a square, using the full length of the rope lying on the ground next to them. Give them no further instructions.

There's no trick. It's just great to see who takes charge, how they organize the corners, if one person facilitates from the middle, and other dynamics that emerge during the activity.

Human Machine

This can be done with large or small groups.

If you have fewer than 10 people, you'll create one machine. If you have more than 10, you'll want to divide into teams of 10 to 20 people and have each team create a machine.

Give participants the following instructions: You are to make a human machine using all of your team members. Choose an appliance, machine, or contraption of any kind, and act out all of its parts with all the members of your team. For example: If you chose an electric toothbrush, several people could lie down to be the handle, while others would be vibrating bristles.

It's best to let groups come up with their own ideas. But here are a few great ones you can suggest if a group seems stuck:

- A pinball machine (with one person rolling around as the ball)

- A ski lift (with participants being scooped up by others with locked arms)

- A washing machine

- A car wash

Sound Effects

Supplies needed: a blank tape and tape recorder or digital recorder for every team.

Instructions: Your group has 15 minutes to record the sounds listed below and any other sounds that they want to add. The sounds must last at least 10 seconds but not more than 15. All members of the group must contribute.

Here's the catch: Teams won't go around and record the real sounds. Instead, teams simulate the sounds themselves. For example, if the list calls for a bunch of barking dogs, the team doesn't go find real dogs. They bark like dogs and record that sound.

Assign each team a different room so they can create the sounds undisturbed.

- Herd of cows

- Cat in a dog kennel

- TV show theme

- Lovesick coyotes on a moonlit night

- A worship song

- Room full of babies

- Traffic

- American Idol® audition

- A typical day in a crowded public bathroom

- A pet dolphin trying to warn his owner that a kid is drowning

- A couple in marriage counseling

Building Interdependence

Objective: If a group of people typically operates independently, use this exercise to help them work interdependently and become a synergistic team.

Copy the following instructions and hand them out to each participant.

- You each have four 5x7 cards. Write one name on each of the cards of the other team members.

- On one side write all the things that you appreciate and admire most about this person.

- On the other side answer this question: "If we are to move from where we are today to became a synergistic, interdependent team, what do I need from this person that I'm not currently getting?" (In other words, what behaviors must this person change if we are to become a high-performance, trusting team?) Be specific.

- Take about 20-30 minutes to fill out the cards. Give each one careful thought.

Now participants give the cards with each person's name to that individual.

Response: When you receive your cards, take 20 minutes to read them carefully and write a response. As you write your response, think of these questions:

- Were you surprised by any of the affirmations on the first side of the card?

- Were you surprised by anything on the second side of the card?

- Are there any recurring themes?

- Are all the team members saying the same thing?

- Does one team member want something totally different from the others?

- What will it mean for you to provide the things requested by other team members?

- Are you willing to make these commitments to the team members, for the sake of the team?

- Be prepared to read or present your response to the other team members.

CASE STUDY: "SYMPTOMS OF STAFF RESISTANCE"

The following case study provides a good training tool for volunteer managers who are struggling with their roles when they have so much else to do. They might feel, "Let's just hire someone to do the job—it would be so much easier."

Or you can use this case study as an example for writing your own case study of a problem that your volunteer managers are struggling with.

To review reasons to include training times with volunteers and staff, go to "Training and Development: A Valuable Tool for Instilling Passion."

Directions:

Training Objective: To discuss the problems of developing an effective volunteer program when the paid staff do not see "volunteer management" as part of the job description."

Training Method: Have each person read the case study and answer the questions at the end of the study (about 4-5 minutes).

If you have more than eight people, divide into groups of four to six people to discuss the case study. Give each group 10-15 minutes to discuss the questions. In groups:

1. Pick a discussion leader

2. Discuss the questions

3. Prepare a report to the class of your answers

If you don't have that many people, then lead the discussion in one group.

Unpacking the Case Study

As groups report back the problems, ask them what can be done. As a leader, you'll learn a lot about what people are feeling regarding the issue of staff resistance. You can also take this opportunity to talk about what you should be doing to help your staff become better volunteer managers.

Case Study

Calvin, a manager in the Centerville City Library, just came back from a meeting of librarians. He's pumped about how many libraries use volunteers to staff many positions. He visited the Huntington Beach City Library and was taken aback by the volunteer room. The volunteers had their own room for processing books. About 15 volunteers were working on the many books, videos, CDs, and DVDs donated to the library. In visiting with one of the volunteers, he found out that more than 100 people volunteer for the library, and the money saved on staff enables the city library to increase hours for the public.

Calvin assigned one of his library employees, Tony, the job of developing a similar volunteer program. Tony was livid. His feeling was, "I'm already six weeks behind and now you want me to recruit, motivate, and manage a bunch of volunteers who won't show up half the time. You've got to be kidding."

Calvin told Tony that if the library didn't start using volunteers, funds could be cut even more. Volunteers provided a way to offer more services to the public. Calvin took on some of Tony's responsibilities and assigned Tony the new task.

Tony gave it his best try, and in six months brought Calvin a request for resources to accomplish their tasks. In order to develop the volunteer program, Tony felt he would need the following resources:

- office/workshop space

- access to telephones, photocopiers, Internet, email

- furniture, stationery, tools, other materials

- prime parking spaces

- special library privileges

Calvin told Tony to make it work, because the volunteer program was working in other libraries. While Tony agreed that the volunteers would bring a lot of enthusiasm into the library, he was afraid of being frustrated. Through his research, he learned that volunteers often didn't show up in libraries that used them. As he went back to his desk he muttered, "Why can't we go back to the good old days when we had plenty of money, a lot of staff, and I didn't have to think about working with volunteers."

Discussion Questions:

- What went wrong? List all of the problems you see in this case study.

- How could the problems have been avoided?

- Just because a volunteer program worked in one county library, will it work in every county library? Defend your answer.

- What insights do you gain about dealing with staff resistance to managing volunteers rather than just hiring the job done?

ENDNOTES

1. Sabrina Tavernise, "Married Couples Are No Longer a Majority, Census Finds," The New York Times (May 26, 2011); retrieved from nytimes.com/2011/05/26/us/26marry.html?_r=1&src=rechp

2. Susan J. Ellis and Katherine H. Campbell, *By The People: A History of Americans as Volunteers* (Philadelphia, PA: Energize, Third Edition, 2005), p. 357

3. dare2share.org/articles/five-adolescent-trends-to-watch-in-2007

4. Miller McPherson, Lynn Smith-Lovin, and Matthew E. Brashears, "Social Isolation in America: Changes in Core Discussion Networks over Two Decades," American Sociological Review (June 2006); retrieved from asanet.org/images/press/docs/pdf/June06ASRFeature.pdf

5. pewinternet.org/Reports/2009/18–Social-Isolation-and-New-Technology.aspx

6. Data for 2002 obtained from worldvolunteerweb.org/fileadmin/docdb/pdf/2006/VIA_fullreport.pdf; data for 2011 obtained from bls.gov/news.release/volun.nr0.htm.

7. Every year the Volunteering in America report (volunteeringinamerica.gov) presents the latest statistics on the state of volunteerism in the United States. The report, released by the Corporation for National and Community Service (nationalservice.gov), is the most comprehensive longitudinal look at volunteering in the United States, spanning over a decade of service data. The information in these paragraphs is a summary of these reports over the past 10 years.

8. *How Young People View Their Lives, Futures and Politics* (Washington, DC: Pew Research Center, 2007); retrieved from people-press.org/reports/pdf/300.pdf

9. mediapost.com/publications/article/170109/turning-on-the-no-collar-workforce.html

10. *Volunteer Growth in America: A Review of Trends Since 1974* (Washington, DC: Corporation for National & Community Service, 2006), 8; retrieved from generosityresearch.nd.edu/assets/13044/volunteer_growth.pdf

11. fastcompany.com/magazine/145/do-something-helping-humanity-with-a-click-of-the-mouse.html

12. inquisitr.com/104197/lady-gaga-headlining-mtv-japan-charity-concert

13. This statistic is found in a February 11, 2010, press release retrieved at redcross.org/portal/site/en/menuitem.94aae3354 70e233f6cf911df43181aa0/?vgnextoid=43ffe0b8da8b6210Vg nVCM10000089f0870aRCRD

14. techcrunch.com/2011/06/20/flurry-time-spent-on-mobile-apps-has-surpassed-web-browsing/

15. fastcompany.com/1742592/are-you-m-ready

16. lyricstime.com/paul-mccartney-when-i-m-64-lyrics.html

17. us.imdb.com/name/nm0005200/

18. *Health, United States, 2006* (Washington, DC: U.S. Department of Health and Human Services, 2006); retrieved from cdc.gov/nchs/data/hus/hus06.pdf#027.

19. volunteeringinamerica.gov/special/Millennials-(born-1982-or-after)

20. Neil Howe and William Strauss, *Millennials Rising: The Next Great Generation* (New York, NY: Vintage Books, 2000), 46.

21. Ibid., 214.

22. *Generation M2: Media in the Lives of 8- to 18-Year-Olds* (Menlo Park, CA: The Henry J. Kaiser Family Foundation, 2010) 34; retrieved from kff.org/entmedia/upload/8010.pdf

23. *Generation M: Media in the Lives of 8- to 18-Year-Olds* (Menlo Park, CA: The Henry J. Kaiser Family Foundation, 2005) 39; retrieved from kff.org/entmedia/upload/Executive-Summary-Generation-M-Media-in-the-Lives-of-8-18-Year-olds.pdf

24. twitchspeed.com/site/article.html

25. ypulse.com/five-more-teen-trends-for-2007

26. us_2011DeloitteVolunteerIMPACTSurvey_datatable_060311.pdf; retrieved from deloitte.com/view/en_US/us/About/Community-Involvement/volunteerism/impact-day/f98eec97e6650310VgnVCM2000001b56f00aRCRD.htm

27. Chap Clark, *Hurt: Inside the World of Today's Teenagers* (Grand Rapids, MI: Baker Books, 2004), 33.

28. Ibid., 75

29. Ibid., 53-54

30. Ibid., 191

31. Ibid., 80

32. mediapost.com/publications/article/170109/turning-on-the-no-collar-workforce.html

33. Bob Nelson, *1001 Ways to Reward Employees* (New York , NY: Workman Publishing Co., 1994), 110.

34. Nancy Austin and Tom Peters, *A Passion for Excellence* (New York, NT: Random House, 1985), 217.

35. Ibid., 217.

36. Ibid., 217.

37. I was watching Peter Vecsey interview Michael Jordan when he came back to basketball after playing baseball, and because I always have a pen and paper handy to write down great quotes that I can use when I speak, I wrote this down and have used it for 20 years because it's a great quote.

38. The original quote is found on page 89 of Covey's book: *"Anytime we think the problem is 'out there' that thought is the problem. We empower what's out there to control us."*

39. Amanda Lenhart, Mary Madden, Aaron Smith, Kristen Purcell, Kathryn Zickuhr, and Lee Rainie, *Teens, Kindness and Cruelty on Social Network Sites* (Washington, DC: Pew Research Center, 2011), 18; retrieved from pewinternet.org/Reports/2011/Teens-and-social-media.aspx

40. *The State of the Media: Mobile Media Report, Q3 2011* (New York, NY: The Nielsen Co., 2011), 2-3; retrieved from nielsen.com/us/en/insights/reports-downloads/2011/state-of-the-media–mobile-media-report-q3-2011.html

41. techcrunch.com/2011/06/20/flurry-time-spent-on-mobile-apps-has-surpassed-web-browsing/

42. Sam Gustin, "Social Media Sparked, Accelerated Egypt's Revolutionary Fire," Wired (February 11, 2011); retrieved from wired.com/epicenter/2011/02/egypts-revolutionary-fire. Quotes from the next few paragraphs of the book also come from this same article.

43. pewinternet.org/Reports/2011/The-Social-Side-of-the-Internet. aspx

44. *The State of the Media: Social Media Report, Q3 2011* (New York, NY: The Nielsen Co., 2011), 1; retrieved from nielsen.com/us/en/insights/reports-downloads/2011/social-media-report-q3. html

45. faithnews.cc/2010/05/06/nashville-pastors-mobilize-volunteers-aid-through-twitter

46. venturebeat.com/2012/03/27/president-on-pinterest/

47. coyotecommunications.com/stuff/findvv.shtml

48. Susan J. Ellis and Jayne Cravens, *The Virtual Volunteering Guidebook* (Palo Alto, CA: ImpactOnline, Inc., 2000), 1. This full-color PDF book can be downloaded for free at serviceleader.org/virtual/guidebook. We recommend it highly for everything you want to know about adding technology and virtual volunteering.

49. habitat.org/how/mission_statement.aspx

50. girlscouts.org/who_we_are/facts/

51. www.prideindustries.com/?navId=20

52. betterworkplacenow.com/qanda1.html

53. James C. Collins and Jerry I. Porras, *Built to Last* (New York, NY: HarperCollins, 1994), 94.

54. Ibid., 97

55. Ellis and Cravens, *The Virtual Volunteering Guidebook*, 35.

56. Used by permission, California Society of Association Executives